In memory of Sally B. Collard

1995

CARS:

An Environmental Challenge

CARS: An Environmental Challenge

Terri Willis
and Wallace B. Black

Educational Consultant
Helen J. Challand, Ph.D.
Professor of Science Education, National-Louis University

Technical Consultant
Deborah Gordon
Director of Transportation, Union of Concerned Scientists

CHILDRENS PRESS®
CHICAGO

A production of B&B Publishing, Inc.

Project Editor: Jean Blashfield Black
Designer: Elizabeth B. Graf
Cover Design: Margrit Fiddle

Artist: Diane Hamil
Production Manager: Dave Conant
Photo Researchers: Marjorie Benson
Kathy Brooks Parker

 Printed on Evergreen Gloss
50% recycled preconsumer waste
Binder's board made from 100% recycled material

Library of Congress Cataloging-in-Publication Data

Willis, Terri and Black, Wallace B.
    Cars — an environmental challenge / Terri Willis and Wallace B. Black
        p.   cm. — (Saving planet earth)
    Includes index.
    Summary: Discusses the environmental damage and safety problems
associated with the internal combustion engine, with an emphasis on emissions
and air pollution, and examines various solutions and alternatives to the
situation.
    ISBN 0-516-05504-6
    1. Automobiles—Motors—Exhaust gas—Environmental aspects—Juvenile
literature. 2. Air—Pollution—Juvenile literature. 3. Transportation, Automotive—Environmental aspects—Juvenile literature. [1. Automobiles—Motors—
Exhaust gas—Environmental aspects. 2. Air—Pollution. 3. Pollution]
I. Black, Wallace B.   II. Title.   III. Series.
    TD886.5.B57   1992
    363.73'1—dc20

                                                        92-9797
                                                          CIP
                                                          AC

Cover photo—© Imtek Imagineering/Masterfile

TABLE OF CONTENTS

Chapter 1

"... It Only Hurts
When You Breathe"

IT WAS A NORMAL WEEKDAY in Mexico City, but 9 million children in the world's biggest city stayed home from school. Almost half of the city's 3 million cars and trucks were ordered off the streets. And thousands of factories were ordered to cut production or even shut down for the day.

On that tragic Tuesday—March 10, 1992—Mexico City faced the most serious air-pollution alert in its history. The pollution levels were four times worse than the safety limit set by the government.

A heavy haze hung over the entire valley in which the giant city is located. Individuals who had to continue working in the open air wore face masks to filter out the pollutants. Oxygen tanks were positioned at key points throughout the city for people who experienced difficulty breathing. Hospital emergency rooms were crowded with people suffering from severe breathing problems—even heart attacks—caused by lack of oxygen. The giant city was sick, and it was making many of its residents sick, too!

It wasn't always like this. . . .

The Beautiful Valley of Mexico

On a clear day in Mexico City one can look to the southeast and enjoy a spectacular view. The three snow-capped peaks of Ixtacihuatl, an inactive volcano, glisten in the sunlight. For centuries, people have enjoyed the natural beauty and pleasant climate of the great Valley of Mexico.

Mexico City is huge—the largest city in the world. It is the home of more than 15 million people, and another 10 million live in the surrounding valley. At 7,500 feet (2,300 meters) above sea level, the valley is cool for most of the year even though it lies in the tropics. The area is like a huge bowl, surrounded by mountains on all sides. Blessed with bountiful harvests from nearby farms, abundant water, and a large labor supply, the city has been Mexico's center of government and industry for more than 700 years.

Mexico City is also the nation's hub for business, education, and the arts. Modern skyscrapers stand side by side with ruins left by Aztec peoples who lived in the area for many centuries. Beautiful palaces and other buildings built during the past 200 years house government offices today.

The very wealthy and a substantial middle class enjoy life in this beautiful city. However, as in any city, there are also many poor people. They come to Mexico City by the millions seeking work and a better life. Instead, they find poverty in the shantytowns and sickness from polluted air.

Mexico City was once a desirable place to live. But those days are gone. A great plague has infected this huge metropolis, bringing disease and death. The great sickness is air pollution—the poisonous outpourings of thousands of factories and millions of cars, buses, and trucks.

Unhampered Growth is to Blame

As this beautiful city grew over the past century, it became a center of industry as well as government. People who could not make a living in the countryside flocked to the city seeking work. As workers came to the city, more factories moved there, too. By the 1980s, the city was inundated with thousands of factories belching out pollutants.

Mexico City's growing population demanded transportation. By 1990, Mexico City had a growing fleet of 15,000 out-of-date buses that continue to emit clouds of smoke for every

mile they move. Some 40,000 poorly maintained taxis and 3 million automobiles also jam the city's streets. All of these contribute to the cloud of scum or *nata*, as the people call the brown cloud of polluted air that hangs over the city.

This vast armada of gasoline- and oil-guzzling vehicles spews out emissions—poisonous gases and dust-like particles. Factories, through corrupt practices and poor law enforcement, contribute to the problem.

In addition, many of the motor vehicles are old and poorly maintained. They burn leaded gasoline, and they are not equipped with antipollution devices, which cars in the United States have been required to have since the 1970s.

Nature Plays a Key Role

Because Mexico City sits at such a high altitude, there is less oxygen in the air than in such a city as New York, which is at sea level. As a result, gasoline and oil do not burn efficiently. So Mexican motor vehicles emit many unburned gases and solids that pollute the air.

The cool air from the mountains that surround Mexico City keeps the polluted air trapped close to the ground. On

Automobile exhaust is responsible for more than three-fourths of the cloud of air pollution that hangs over Mexico City.

9

calm, cool days, atmospheric conditions called thermal inversions hold down the *nata* that hurts every living thing in the valley.

And It's All Breathed In

Among the emissions are hydrocarbons (numerous compounds made up of hydrogen and carbon) and nitrogen oxides. In the presence of sunlight, these chemicals react with the oxygen in the air to make *ozone*, a form of oxygen that can irritate our eyes and limit the amount of the right kind of oxygen we get.

The World Health Organization has set standards for the amount of ozone that can safely be in the air without harming the ability of people to breathe. In 1991, Mexico City's air exceeded those standards on 300 days out of 365.

Prolonged exposure to excess ozone causes damage to the respiratory system. Children, pregnant women, and elderly people are particularly vulnerable. But people can't stop breathing when the ozone concentration is too high.

Every year some 100,000 deaths are caused by the city's pollution. Almost three-fourths of Mexico City's newborn babies suffer from respiratory problems or dangerous levels of lead from engine exhaust in their blood.

Respiratory problems are very common among young children and babies when the amount of ozone in the air is very high. A majority of newborns in Mexico City have damaged respiratory systems.

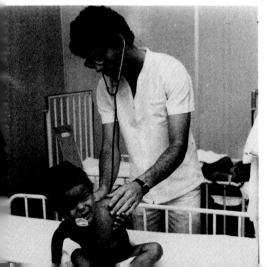

Taking Steps

Although pollution comes from many sources, natural as well as man-made, almost 80 percent of Mexico City's pollution comes from gasoline- and oil-burning motor vehicles. In 1991, they spewed out 4,356,000 tons (3,952,000 metric tons) of pollutants in Mexico City.

The government of President Carlos Salinas de Gortari has taken giant steps to combat pollution. Hundreds of factories, including a huge General Motors plant, are being forced to move out of the Valley of Mexico. Public transportation is being increased and improved.

Even in Moscow, Russia, where it's difficult for individuals to own cars, auto emissions contribute heavily to the smog that fouls the city's air.

But as the numbers of people and their vehicles increase, the problem continues to grow.

Mexico City is Not Alone

Pollution, traffic congestion, and related problems are found in cities such as Athens, Greece; São Paulo, Brazil; Cairo, Egypt; Manila, the Philippines; Bangkok, Thailand; New Delhi, India; and even in the most advanced cities of the world—London, Paris, and Berlin. And in the United States, over 100 cities exceed safe standards of ozone levels for part of the year. Los Angeles in particular suffers many of the same problems as Mexico City.

Yes, it does "hurt when you breathe" polluted air. And most of that polluted air comes from cars and trucks and their related industries.

The automobile represents one of the greatest achievements of the modern world. It is a great blessing in many ways. We've come to depend on our vehicles. We have reached the point where society cannot live without the automobile and yet we cannot live safely with it.

Are the 550 million cars on our planet an environmental menace or an environmental challenge? That question can only be answered by all of us working together.

Chapter 2

The Great
Love Affair

F. C. BRINK

Supreme in Service
as in Saving

THE Ford car, with its uniformly dependable service, its comfort and convenience, gives a key to the wide and healthful out-of-doors. It enables the owner—her family and friends—to have all the benefits of fresh air and change of scene, without fatigue.

And when it is a question of cost, a Ford is acknowledged, the world over, to set a standard of value that has never been approached. For not only is it the least expensive car to buy, but the most economical to operate.

RUNABOUT, $260; TOURING, $290; COUPE, $520; TUDOR SEDAN, $580; FORDOR SEDAN, $660. All Prices F. O. B. Detroit
On Open Cars Starter and Demountable Rims $85 Extra
Full-Size Balloon Tires Optional at an Extra Cost of $25

FORD MOTOR COMPANY, DETROIT, MICHIGAN

THE UNIVERSAL CAR

MAKE SAFETY YOUR RESPONSIBILITY

IN HUNDREDS OF FACTORIES, in more than a dozen countries around the world, motor vehicles are being designed and manufactured.

As the big machines roll down assembly lines, skilled workers standing alongside complete their tasks. One person tightens a screw, another sets a tire in place, still another directs a robot welder. In assembly-line fashion, nearly 14,000 parts—fenders, gears, switches, lights, and more—are joined together in a smooth symphony. In only a few hours, an automobile or truck rolls off the line, and another object of our affection is born.

Nearly everybody likes a shiny, fast, new car—especially Americans. Ever since Henry Ford's Model Ts rolled off the assembly line, cars have been driving Americans wild with enthusiasm. Today, nearly every household in the United States owns at least one motor vehicle.

Ford's cars weren't the first automobiles, but they were the first to create a stir across an entire nation. Before that, cars were mostly the toys of the wealthy few.

Early Autos

The first automobile was built in 1769 by a Frenchman, Nicolas-Joseph Cugnot. It didn't look much like the cars of today, but it was still an automobile. An automobile is actually any vehicle that moves under its own power—that isn't pushed or pulled by some other force.

Designed to help carry artillery into battle, Cugnot's automobile had three wheels and was powered by steam. Hot steam was released from a boiler into a cylinder against a piston. The piston was linked to the wheels, which turned. Cugnot's vehicle carried four people, but its top speed was only 2.25 miles (3.6 kilometers) per hour. It could operate for only about 20 minutes before running out of steam.

Most of the vehicles that followed during the next century were also powered by steam. Steam cars were smelly and noisy, and the possibility of a boiler explosion made them dangerous, too.

In 1876, German engineer Nikolaus August Otto invented an engine that was powered by gasoline instead of steam. It was similar to the one found in most modern cars, but it didn't catch on until after the turn of the century. Instead, electric cars gained in popularity. They beat both gasoline and steam on several counts—they were quieter, more reliable, and started instantly. However, they could travel only about 30 to 40 miles (48 to 64 kilometers) before their bulky storage batteries had to be recharged.

FACT

In 1900, there were about 125,000 cars produced in the United States. Nearly 40 percent of them were powered by electricity, another 40 percent were powered by steam, and only about 20 percent ran on gasoline.

Before Henry Ford's popularity skyrocketed with the introduction of the Model T, he experimented with several other cars, including this quadcycle, built in 1896.

Gasoline-Powered Cars

Eventually, motor vehicle designers realized that gasoline engines were not only safer than steam, but they also enabled cars to travel faster and longer distances.

The gasoline engine got another popularity boost in the mid-1800s when advances in technology made the fuel easier to obtain. Within a few years, oil was being drilled around the world, with the United States, Europe, the Middle East, and the East Indian islands leading the way. Techniques for refining oil—separating crude oil into various products, especially gasoline—soon followed.

Today's gasoline engines, called internal combustion engines, are far more efficient and dependable than the early versions, but the basic principles are still the same.

The first commercial oil well in the United States was drilled in 1859 in Titusville, Pennsylvania, by E. L. Drake, shown here on the right.

How a Gasoline Engine Works. In a typical automobile gasoline engine there are 4 to 8 steel or aluminum tubes, called cylinders. Two small holes at the top of each cylinder are sealed by valves—the intake valve and the exhaust valve. Another opening contains a spark plug.

The piston is a shorter tube that fits snugly inside the cylinder. At the bottom of the piston, a connecting rod connects the piston to the crankshaft.

When the car is running, the piston moves up and down in a sequence called a four-stroke cycle. On the first stroke, the intake valve opens briefly, allowing a mixture of air and gasoline to enter the cylinder. The piston moves up, compressing the air and gasoline into a very dense, explosive

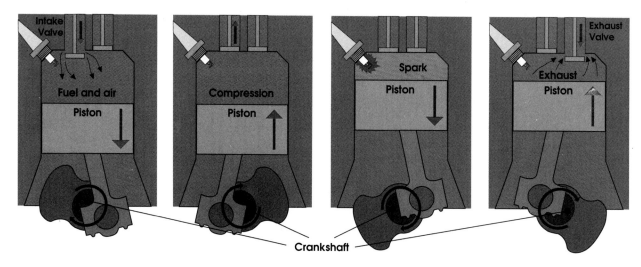

Crankshaft

What Makes a Car Move?

Inside each cylinder of a gasoline engine (above) is a piston and two valves—an intake and an exhaust valve. As the intake valve opens, it allows in a mixture of gasoline and air. This mixture is compressed when the piston moves up and is ignited by a spark from a spark plug. The explosion forces the piston back downward and then up, forcing the exhaust gases out through the exhaust valve. These gases eventually exit through the exhaust pipe.

This process happens repeatedly in each cylinder, sending the pistons rapidly up and down. The rise and fall of the pistons cause the crankshaft to move round. The crankshaft is attached to the transmission—a series of gears that slows the motion to a reasonable driving speed (see below). The driveshaft then transfers the spinning motion to the differential, another set of gears, that causes the axle to rotate. Two wheels are attached to the axle, and as it goes round, the car moves. The other two wheels do not receive power except in a 4-wheel-drive vehicle.

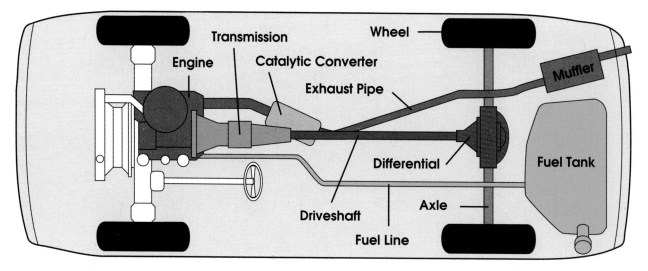

mixture. The spark plug then creates a spark, which causes the mixture to explode. The explosion forces the piston and the connecting rod down, causing the crankshaft to rotate. The rotation of the crankshaft is transmitted to the wheels through a series of gears, causing the car to move forward.

The crankshaft also pushes the connecting rod and piston back up to the top of the cylinder, where the exhaust valve opens, allowing the escape of the chemical by-products left behind after the explosion of the air-and-gas mixture. Those by-products cause air pollution.

The motion of the crankshaft also coordinates the opening and closing of the valves, so that the entire process flows in an orderly manner.

And what is it that gets the whole process going in the first place? You simply turn the key in the ignition, which signals the battery to release some of its stored electricity. The electricity flows to an electric starter motor that, through a number of steps, causes the first rotation of the crankshaft. From there, the four-stroke cycle repeats itself thousands of times per minute.

The Gasoline Engine Comes of Age

Auto manufacturing on a large scale got underway at the turn of the century in Europe when Germans Gottlieb Daimler and Carl Benz both started their own companies, which later merged. They improved the early gasoline engines, making them more powerful and efficient.

In the United States, automotive pioneers included Ransom Eli Olds and Alexander and James Packard, and many others were eager to join the parade. Over the coming years their names would come and go.

In 1898, 50 companies produced automobiles in the United States. By 1908, that number had grown to 241. However, in 1909, when American manufacturers built 124,000 cars, more than 2 million horse-drawn carriages were also produced.

Early cars were not very reliable—brakes gave out, tires fell off, and engines could stall at any moment. No one could depend on an auto for any important journey, so they were mostly recreational vehicles for the wealthy few.

Toys for the Rich. At first, cars were mainly a curiosity. Drivers had to put up with roads designed for animals, carriages, and pedestrians—certainly not cars. People were frightened by the noisy, sputtering machines. In Vermont, laws required someone to walk in front of the car waving a red flag, to warn others of what was coming!

An article that appeared in a 1907 issue of *Country Life* spoke of the pleasures of piercing the darkness of night while driving after sundown, but it also cautioned drivers who did so. They should be prepared, at any moment, to stop and calm the horses of any oncoming carriage by throwing their lap robes over their headlights.

While the fanciest cars cost about $7,000, some basic models could be had for $500. This was still quite a large sum of money at that time, but not totally out of reach for some working people. But it wasn't only their initial cost that kept cars out of the hands of average people, it was also the costs of upkeep.

Limited Use. Cars did not catch on in cities as well as they did in rural areas. Most cities in the early 1900s had streetcar and trolley systems that made getting around quick and easy. People lived in close-knit neighborhoods near work, shopping, and schools. And for long-distance travel, railroads fit the bill.

The most obvious use for motor vehicles within cities was to transport goods—a job previously done by horses. Trucks were faster and more efficient—cleaner, too.

When cars were first introduced, they shared crowded city streets with pedestrians, horses, and trolleys, as this Chicago scene shows.

According to historian James Flink, "In New York City alone at the turn of the century, horses deposited on the streets every day an estimated 2.5 million pounds (1.1 million kilograms) of manure and 60,000 gallons (227,000 liters) of urine, accounting for about two-thirds of the filth that littered the city's streets. Excreta from the horses in the form of dried dust irritated nasal passages and lungs, then became a syrupy mass to wade through and track into the home whenever it rained."

Ford Revolutionizes Life

Henry Ford can be credited with turning the car from a luxury into a near-necessity. He devised a system of producing autos that made them reliable, easy to maintain, and inexpensive. His popular Model T of 1908 forever changed the way Americans, Canadians, and the rest of the world would travel.

Ford revolutionized the way cars were built in 1913 when he introduced the assembly line. As the machines traveled

The Model T assembly line, shown here in 1914, changed the way cars were built, making them cheap enough for many people to afford.

along a conveyor belt, each worker stationed along the line installed only one or two pieces. Each person performed his same small job on hundreds of cars every day. Auto manufacturing was suddenly cheaper and faster, with consistent quality.

The cars were priced so that many people could afford them—about $400—and they didn't require as much maintenance as the cars of the past. By 1914, there were 2 million cars in the United States, and during the next 15 years, that number exploded to 20 million. Nearly half the nation's families owned a car.

Roadways were improved to meet the growing needs of motorists. Though less than one-tenth of the country's roads were surfaced in 1909, two decades later a huge system of concrete highways connected most parts of the nation. Citizens paid for these improvements with taxes on gasoline. Never before had people seemed so willing to contribute to government spending.

Vehicle manufacturing became the major industry in the

Interior trim is installed on vehicles as they roll down an assembly line. Nearly 50 million cars are built each year. Japan produces the most, about 13 million, followed by the United States, with 11 million.

United States. Many smaller automakers fell by the wayside, as the strongest companies emerged. By 1970, the "Big Three" U.S. carmakers—Ford, Chrysler, and General Motors—manufactured nearly all American cars. Today, Japanese cars, such as Honda, Toyota, Nissan, Isuzu, and Mitsubishi, are taking a large share of the American market. Germany also builds many cars sold in North America, including Volkswagen, Mercedes Benz, and Audi. Most recently, Korea has joined the market with Hyundai.

The Car Craze

The "Roaring Twenties" gave the automobile a real boost. Along with the growth in the car industry came changes in the way Americans lived. Cars became a symbol of "the good life." People wanted to travel farther and faster, for work and for pleasure.

In the 1920s, cars such as the Stutz Bearcat, Packard, and Cadillac roadsters and open touring cars were symbols of success. Automobile races, such as the Indianapolis 500, which was first run in 1911, increased public awareness of the automobile.

People were working fewer hours and cars made it easy to get away for vacations, or even for an afternoon picnic. Families could make short or long trips on a moment's notice—they didn't have to wait for public transportation.

The Great Depression of the 1930s and World War II (1939-1945) combined to slow the American economy and the rate of auto ownership. Still, the seed had been planted. Families gave up other things in order to buy cars. And in the late 1940s, when the financial picture brightened, the car came to symbolize the "American Dream."

Canadian Cars

In some aspects, Canada's history with cars closely parallels that of the United States. When automobiles first appeared on the scene in Canada in 1867, they drew very little interest.

However, Canada's lack of interest may have been partly due to the fact that the first steam buggy, built by Henry Seth Taylor of Stanstead, Quebec, broke down during its initial demonstration at the Stanstead Fair. Taylor continued working to improve his automobile, until one day he had a disastrous crash at the bottom of a steep hill. He'd never considered brakes for his vehicle! So Taylor gave up, closing the chapter on Canada's first car.

Little else happened until the turn of the century when many small car manufacturers responded to the growing excitement about cars. But since the Canadian population is about one-tenth that of the United States, it was difficult for a Canadian carmaker to survive selling just to Canadians.

The companies that did best were those that worked with American firms. One of the first successful joint arrangements was the incorporation of the Ford Motor Company of Canada Ltd., in 1904. Business really took off in 1908, with the advent of the Model T, which had the same phenomenal impact on Canada as it had on the United States.

More joint ventures followed. The parts were often produced in the United States, where they could be made in large numbers for less money. Then the cars were assembled in Canada.

In urban areas through-out Canada and the United States, cars grew in popularity as mass-transit systems fell out of favor with the public. Most city adminis-trators worked to make car travel more effective, rather than to improve mass transit.

Automobiles caught hold in Canada as quickly as they did in the United States, and soon most roadways, such as this one in Toronto, were filled with cars and trucks.

Still, some cars were strictly Canadian-made. The Canada Cycle and Motor Company, for example, began producing a fine-quality vehicle called the Russell in 1905. This firm's truck designs later served as the basis for early armored vehicles used during World War I (1914-1918). Eventually, though, this company closed, along with the hundreds of other carmakers around the world that saw their rapid rise and fall in the early years of cars.

Today, several automakers have plants in Canada, including the Big Three, as well as the European Volvo and the Japanese Isuzu, Toyota, and Honda.

The Dream Reaches Its Peak

Woody Guthrie, a great folk singer of the 1940s, sang of "the ribbon of highway" that stretched across the United States in his song, "This Land is Your Land." Many people felt that cars and trucks, as well as the roadways built to accommodate them, were signs of all that was right with the country—freedom, wealth, independence, and manufacturing superiority.

Few people were interested in traveling long distances by train anymore—cars were just as cheap, and they offered more freedom. Most of the passenger railway system died. Coal, oil, and heavy manufactured goods are still carried by trains, but, increasingly, the trucking industry has taken over much of the railroads' business.

The Changing Shape of Cities

Before the automobile was invented, most wealthy businessmen preferred to live near their work in the heart of the city. Public transportation and chauffeured carriages took them to and from work. When cars made traveling even easier, the wealthy were free to move to the more spacious outskirts of town. Suburbia was born.

The middle class and the poor people remained in the city. They usually didn't own cars, so they had to rely on mass transit systems to get them around. And as more poor people moved toward the city centers, governments devoted fewer resources to their upkeep, turning more inner-city areas into slums.

The Interstate Highway System, established in 1956, proved how important cars had become. By 1973, the United States was spending more than $5 billion in federal funds on highways each year, creating the most extensive system in the world—42,500 miles (68,400 kilometers) long.

Cities deteriorated further when expressways were built to handle the growing numbers of cars coming from the suburbs. Many highways were built through once-healthy neighborhoods and over parks. These roadways ruined housing and damaged the neighborhoods' appearance. Federal, state, and city governments spent money on roads, letting public transportation degrade.

Roads were built by manual labor prior to World War II, but machines soon did much of the hard work. Technology has made it possible to build plenty of roads to meet the needs of motorists. But not everybody likes all that asphalt.

In the late 1950s and 1960s, some people began to say "No" to more highways. In California, where pavement threatened to cover much of the landscape, community groups formed to stop the development. A group in San Francisco was successful in stopping the completion of the Embarcadero freeway, and in 1966, it convinced the city to reject more than $240 million in federal highway aid—an un-heard-of rejection.

In most instances, though, the millions of avid car owners, along with the huge automotive and oil industries, won any disagreements. Today, more money is spent on interstate, state, and city highways than ever before.

Automobiles made it possible for wealthy people to move out of city centers, away from their work, while poor people, who couldn't afford cars, moved into the city cores, where they often live near the factories.

Autos against the Air

Following World War II, some environment-minded people began to blame automobiles for the smog that was making the air unbreathable in some areas. Again, California took the lead. In Los Angeles, large numbers of cars and trucks spewed emissions into the air, and the mountains surrounding the city kept the fumes from spreading out and away from the area. California passed its first law calling for a curb on vehicle emissions in 1960.

At first, automakers tried to say that there was no smog problem. Later they agreed there was a problem but said any solution would be very costly.

In the meantime, as the number of motor vehicles throughout the world continued to mount, so did the air-pollution problems. The lead from gasoline, released in tailpipe emissions, was considered a major culprit. The federal government passed the Motor Vehicle Air Pollution Act of 1965, which called for leaded gasoline to be phased out. It also set limits on the amount of emissions cars could produce. The Federal Clean Air Act, passed five years later, lowered those amounts further.

During the 1970s, the oil and auto industries began to respond. The oil industry worked to deliver fuels that would reduce pollution. Automakers built more fuel-efficient cars and added devices called catalytic converters to reduce harmful emissions.

Technology has simplified road-building. Huge bulldozers and graders clear and level land, and modern paving machines can lay 1 mile (1.6 kilometers) of asphalt in a single day.

Though California has had air-pollution laws in effect for more than three decades, the huge numbers of cars that clog Los Angeles roadways (left) *still cause dangerous smog to hang over the city* (right) *many days each year.*

But the public had to play a role, too. People had to make the choice to cut down driving and to drive more efficient cars that created less pollution. Yet no matter what problems cars caused, it seemed that many Americans wouldn't give up their best-loved vehicles of choice—the gas-guzzlers.

To meet the demand, the Big Three carmakers continued to turn out big cars with lots of chrome and lots of horse-power. Along with foreign manufacturers, they also made more affordable and fuel-efficient cars that appealed to a limited segment of people in the United States. But it took a crisis to shake up most Americans.

The Arab Oil Embargo

In 1973, the Arab members of the Organization of Petroleum Exporting Countries (OPEC) launched an embargo on oil flowing into the United States, meaning that shipments were cut back dramatically. This caught the country off guard. The nation had become heavily dependent on cheap foreign oil. When the supply was cut back, long lines formed at gas stations and prices quadrupled.

Quickly, people realized that efficient cars used less gasoline, and that driving slower (an average of 55 miles or

88 kilometers per hour) also used less gasoline. Most big American-made cars got about 14 miles per gallon (mpg) (6 kilometers per liter [kpl]), so the smaller, efficient foreign cars became popular. Congress, meanwhile, imposed a law that required U.S. automakers to reach a level for new cars of 27.5 mpg (11 kpl), but it gave them ten years, until 1985, to meet this new standard.

People who had access to mass transit systems also began to use them instead of driving. Federal, state, and local governments throughout the country funded programs to boost the efficiency of buses and light rail systems. Research into electric-powered cars increased. People swore that we must never again be so dependent on foreign oil.

Forgotten Lessons. Eventually, the oil embargo was lifted, and as the supply of gasoline increased, its cost went down. Most Americans soon forgot the lessons they had learned. The number of cars on American roads increased at an average annual rate of 2.4 percent from 1970 to 1987, and trucks showed an annual increase of 6 percent during that time. Congestion on highways grew worse, even as new roadways filled the landscape.

A second oil crisis occurred in 1978-79, when Iran cut off oil imports to the United States during the Iranian Revolu-

Gasoline pumps were often closed at stations throughout the United States during the Arab oil embargo.

tion. Again, prices rose and lines formed at gas pumps. Americans' renewed awareness of fuel efficiency lasted until 1982, when the oil prices dropped to record lows.

The administration of President Ronald Reagan (1980-1988) relaxed the gas-mileage restrictions on U.S. automakers, and once again, large, powerful, polluting gas-guzzlers became popular. The country's dependence on foreign sources of oil increased.

An Earth Experience

Cut Down on Your Travel

What are the transportation habits in your family? For two weeks, keep careful records of each time the car leaves the garage. Record the mileage by reading the odometer before and after the trip. Record the purpose for the trip. If your family owns two cars, collect data on both. Also record the number of gallons and the cost of the gasoline purchased during these two weeks. What percentage of your household budget goes for transportation?

Now it is time to sit down with your family members to figure out ways to reduce gasoline consumption. Which trips were unnecessary? Were there times when one of you could have walked or ridden a bicycle instead of taking the car? Can you car pool with a neighbor when going shopping or to school? Can you get everything you need in one trip every week instead of driving daily? Can you take public transportation?

You and your family may not be aware you are wasting gas. Discuss it as a budget problem as well as an environmental issue. Change your transportation habits to help save money, reduce air pollution, and save one of our dwindling nonrenewable natural resources—petroleum.

When Iraq invaded Kuwait in 1990, the United States rushed to protect the tiny, oil-rich nation. Officially, the military was there to protect Kuwait's independence. But many people believe that the real reason troops were sent to fight in the Persian Gulf War was to protect a source of oil.

Too Many Cars

Cars and trucks are a driving force behind much of North America's history. They have helped to make us mobile and economically strong. But they have also caused problems.

If we don't change the way we use cars—and quickly—the damage will far exceed the benefit. But the average American is not ready to change.

George Ivey, Jr., a Georgia official, summed it up: "The automobile is as American as apple pie, but just like eating too much apple pie will make you sick, too many cars on our roads and streets degrade our quality of life."

During the Persian Gulf War of 1991, hundreds of Kuwait's oil wells were set afire by Iraqi troops. They burned out of control for months.

Chapter 3

Auto Pollution Aplenty

CARS BEGIN TO POLLUTE our planet long before their tires hit the road and continue well past the cars' cruising days. Pollution is created while cars are built, more pollutants spew out every minute they're on the road, and cars continue to pollute while they rust away in junkyards.

Gas and Oil—The Main Culprits

Cars cause several kinds of pollution, and the most serious kind is one of the most obvious. We see the clouds of gray smoke that follow some cars down the freeway and we smell the gassy fumes. Caught in heavy traffic, we sometimes get a dizzy headache, itching eyes, or a tightened throat. These are all the results of emissions—the horrible stuff that blows out of the tailpipe of every car powered by gas and oil. But most of the time we don't even notice—or simply ignore—these problems.

Exhaust emissions are chemical compounds left over after the fuel and air has burned in the cylinders.

Emissions from cars and trucks contribute as much as 80 percent of the total air pollution in such highly polluted areas as Mexico City and Los Angeles.

An average motor vehicle in the United States consumes about 690 gallons (2,612 liters) of gasoline each year. Passenger cars burn about 500 gallons (1,893 liters) of gasoline each, while trucks use about 1,350 gallons (5,110 liters), usually of diesel fuel, each year.

FACT

While all gasoline-powered cars create emissions, some cars—particularly big, old, broken-down ones—really spew out a lot of filthy fumes. The exhaust from this car blows out from the bottom, since the tailpipe has rusted off.

The basic ingredients that create the emissions are gasoline and the oxygen necessary to make it burn. Gasoline is processed from crude oil, a fossil fuel that was formed over millions of years by the compression of ancient plants and animals. It is the same process that made coal.

Gasoline is composed of liquid hydrocarbons (HC) and small amounts of sulfur (S), plus other trace elements. Air is made up of 78 percent nitrogen (N), 21 percent oxygen (O), and 1 percent argon and other elements. Water vapor (H_2O), also present in air, is made up of hydrogen (H) and oxygen. A certain amount of solid particles, called particulates, such as dust, are also suspended in the air.

All these ingredients are present in the engine's cylinders, and all of them are changed as the gasoline burns. Since emissions are created in the process of burning fuel but don't actually help power the car, they are considered *by-products.*

They exit the exhaust valves as a number of harmful chemical compounds. The main exhaust emissions are carbon monoxide (CO), carbon dioxide (CO_2), hydrocarbons, nitrogen oxides (NO_x), sulfur dioxide (SO_2), and suspended particulates, such as soot that hangs in the air.

For every gallon (3.8 liters) of gasoline they burn, cars produce about 20 pounds (9 kilograms) of carbon dioxide, one of the principal tailpipe emissions. The average car on the road gets approximately 20 miles per gallon (8.5 kilometers per liter) and makes 1 pound of CO_2 for each mile (0.8 kilogram per kilometer).

Similar emissions are also the by-product of the diesel engine—another kind of engine widely used in trucks. The diesel engine has no spark plug. Instead, it compresses air so much that it heats enough to explode when the fuel is injected into the cylinder. Again, fumes are released into the air in great quantities through exhaust systems.

Pollution Problems. These exhaust chemicals can cause health problems for people, other animals, and plants. They even cause buildings and statues to disintegrate!

See the chart on page 37 to learn more about these harmful compounds and the effects they cause.

One harmful chemical that was once common in gasoline—lead—is no longer present in most gasoline sold in the

Dr. Donald Stedman of the University of Denver demonstrates his remote sensor, which can detect excessive levels of hydrocarbon emissions from cars as they drive by.

United States and Canada. Lead used to be added to gasoline because it helped gasoline burn more completely, thus reducing "engine knocking," and it also improved an engine's power.

But in the mid-1960s, it was discovered that lead from emissions caused serious health problems for people and animals. Today, lead is still found in the so-called "regular" gasoline that must be used in cars produced before 1970. It is also still widely used in many foreign countries.

A Dangerous Mix

These exhaust emissions are not only harmful on their own, but they mix with each other and with other chemicals in the atmosphere to cause additional harm.

Ozone (O_3) is created when sunlight causes pollutants in the air, especially NO_x from gasoline, to react. In the lower atmosphere, where it's known as smog, ozone is a harmful pollutant. Interestingly, though, a different sort of ozone at the upper level of the atmosphere keeps people healthy. As a thin layer in the stratosphere, this ozone, created by natural processes, prevents the dangerous ultraviolet rays in sunlight from reaching the Earth.

Ozone is composed of three oxygen atoms. It has a slight odor that some people call an "electrical" smell and can be seen as smog. High concentrations of ozone can cause severe respiratory problems, and are especially dangerous to the lungs and hearts of the very young and the elderly.

Ozone is particularly severe in cities such as Mexico City and Los Angeles, where mountains and local weather phenomena trap the polluted air close to the ground.

Emissions	About the Emissions	Effects
CARBON MONOXIDE	Nearly all of the world's CO pollution is caused by motor vehicles—as much as 82 percent in major urban areas. About 67 million tons (60.3 million metric tons) of odorless, colorless CO are emitted into the atmosphere each year in the United States.	CO, in high concentrations in enclosed areas, can cause death. In normal outside exposure, especially in cars stalled in heavy traffic, it can cause headaches and place additional stress upon the heart. It interferes with the blood's ability to absorb oxygen, so it hampers perception and thinking, slows reflexes, and causes drowsiness. If inhaled by a pregnant woman, it may threaten the growth and mental development of the unborn baby.
NITROGEN OXIDES	Nitrogen oxides—nitrogen dioxide and nitric oxide—contribute to the heavy brownish haze often seen over congested areas. Motor vehicles create about 43 percent of the nitrogen oxides in the air.	NO_x can cause respiratory infections and lung disease. They may also contribute to bronchitis, pneumonia, emphysema, and cancer. NO_x react with HC in combination with heat and sunlight to create another pollutant, ozone.
HYDRO-CARBONS	HCs are made up of a wide range of different hydrocarbon compounds. Most HCs in the atmosphere come from tailpipe emissions, but others come from the evaporation of gasoline during refueling, gasoline leakage, and poorly maintained fuel systems in older cars.	These gases react with NO_x to form ozone. Some hydrocarbons, such as benzene, are known to cause cancer.
CARBON DIOXIDE	During its lifetime, a car will emit CO_2 approximately equal to the car's weight. There is more CO_2 emitted into the atmosphere than any other emission mentioned here. Cars and trucks are responsible for about 20 percent of the total—the rest comes from power plants, industry, and agriculture.	CO_2 contributes to the greenhouse effect. Many scientists think that too much CO_2 is causing the Earth to heat up.
SULFUR OXIDES	Cars and trucks add only a small amount of SO_x to the air—most are produced by the burning of high sulfur coal to generate electricity and other industrial processes.	SO_x can cause a variety of human health problems. They also combine with moisture in the atmosphere to form acid rain, which damages lakes, forests, and man-made structures throughout North America and Europe.
PARTICULATES	Smoke, ash, and other particles emitted from motor vehicles and industrial plants mix with dust blown up by the wind to make up particulate matter. Diesel engines, which don't completely burn the fuel, contribute transportation's largest share. Cars contribute very little.	Particulate matter hangs as a thick cloud over its surroundings, causing a variety of respiratory problems in humans and impairing visibility.

Exhaust Fumes and Plants

Gasoline-powered vehicles release hazardous wastes into the air constantly. You can find out what effect these gases have on plants. The concentration of these harmful chemicals is 10 to 100 times higher in cities with lots of traffic than in rural areas. This activity will help us test the difference.

Germinate two flats of plants, using seeds from the same packets in both. Include a row each of grass, beans, corn, and marigolds. Water as needed. When the plants are a few inches high, thin the seedlings out until you have five of each kind, evenly spaced, in each flat. Measure and record the height of each plant along with the location of the plant in the flat, so that you can compare its growth later.

Place one flat of growing plants outside a house near a busy highway. Find a spot in the country, away from the pollution of the city, for the second flat. Be sure other variables, such as light and water, are kept constant for both sets of plants. The only factor we are testing is the kind of air in the plants' environments.

After several weeks, remeasure the heights of all the plants. Look for signs of distress. Ozone produces reddish-brown flecks on the upper surface of leaves, and chlorophyll gets bleached out. Brown spots and reduced growth are caused by nitrogen oxides. The effect of these emissions is not as visible in animals, where most of the damage occurs inside their bodies.

What's Being Done? Cars manufactured in North America in recent years have devices on the exhaust systems called catalytic converters. These devices keep some of the pollutants out of the air.

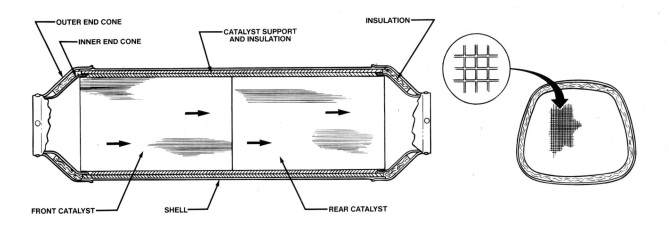

OUTER END CONE

INNER END CONE

CATALYST SUPPORT
AND INSULATION

INSULATION

FRONT CATALYST

SHELL

REAR CATALYST

A catalytic converter consists of an insulated chamber containing pellets of various metal oxides. As the exhaust gases pass through the catalytic converter, the hydrocarbons (HC) and carbon monoxide (CO) combine with the metal oxides. They are converted into water vapor (H_2O) and carbon dioxide (CO_2), reducing the CO and HC pollutants.

Lots of CO_2 is still emitted, however, and that has brought a problem that may be increasing.

Greenhouse Gases

Certain gases trap the sun's heat within the atmosphere and help keep the Earth's temperature warm enough for life. This natural process is called the *greenhouse effect* and the gases are called greenhouse gases.

However, people are now creating more greenhouse gases than are needed to keep the planet's temperature warm, especially by burning gasoline in motor vehicles. More of these gases means that more heat is trapped. Some experts predict that the Earth's average temperature will rise several degrees—enough to cause serious changes in the way the planet and its people live and function. This process is called *global warming*.

Catalytic converters play an important role in making cars more friendly to the environment. Dangerous exhaust gases pass through the catalytic converter and exit as less-harmful gases and water. The catalytic converter contains a honeycomb of precious metals—platinum, palladium, and rhodium—that cause these chemical reactions to occur.

Climate changes from global warming could force changes in the types of crops grown in different places.

The main greenhouse gas is CO_2. Though some of it comes naturally from the environment, cars and trucks are the two largest sources of man-made carbon dioxide. Other greenhouse gases from car and truck tailpipe emissions include ozone and CO.

FACT

Poorly maintained automobiles run "dirty" and contribute a high percentage of emissions, while well-maintained cars pollute less. A test in Illinois showed that 30 percent of the cars on the road run dirty and contribute 80 percent of all emissions.

Other principal greenhouse gases are methane (CH_4) and chlorofluorocarbons (CFCs). Though these don't come from tailpipe emissions, the auto and oil industries help add them to the environment in other ways.

Methane. Methane traps heat better than most other greenhouse gases. Most methane comes from natural gas pipelines, and more is produced when crude oil is processed and refined. Some additional methane is produced by the natural processes in plant and animal life cycles. CO emissions from motor vehicles help increase the methane concentration in our air.

Chlorofluorocarbons. These greenhouse gases were invented in a laboratory. CFCs are complex chemical combinations of carbon, chlorine, and fluorine. One common CFC is known by its trade name, Freon.

Because they do not react easily with other chemicals, CFCs are used to propel other substances out of aerosol spray cans and to produce polystyrene foam—Styrofoam. Freon is used as a cooling agent in refrigerators and air conditioners, including those in cars and trucks. CFCs also help produce the foam for some car seats and are used as solvents in manufacturing and servicing motor vehicles.

CFCs contribute to global warming by trapping heat near the Earth, and they also damage the ozone layer in the stratosphere.

If the pattern of global warming follows the predictions of many scientists, the Earth's average temperature will rise by several degrees over the next few decades. The temperature change will have serious effects on humans, impacting the foods we eat, the way we dress, even where we live.

Most nations recognize that the use of CFCs must be phased out in the automotive industry and elsewhere as soon as possible. Some progress is being made, but it is slow, and real changes won't begin to take effect until after the year 2000.

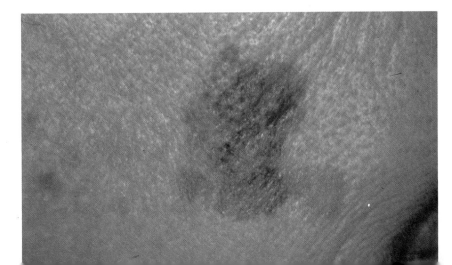

As the ozone layer is weakened by CFCs and other pollutants, people may be more subject to such ailments as sight-damaging cataracts and skin cancer. This patch on a woman's cheek shows an early stage of skin cancer.

41

More Fossil Fuel Problems

Exhaust emissions aren't the only problems created in the mix of gasoline and cars. It takes many steps to get the oil from underground pools into gas tanks, and along the way, a great deal of land, air, and water can be polluted.

Oil Exploration and Drilling. When oil companies explore and drill for crude oil around the world, they damage and pollute the environment. They carve out wide paths through pristine forests to drag in their heavy equipment. They build drilling platforms for offshore wells in fragile ocean ecosystems. They abandon the rusting skeletons of rigs on Arctic tundra. Poisonous chemicals used in drilling leak into the atmosphere, the water, and the land. Plants and animals are often destroyed, and the lives of native peoples are changed forever.

One of the worst oil spills was the Exxon Valdez *disaster in Alaska in 1989. Here, huge booms are used in an attempt to contain the oil, so that it can be cleaned off the water.*

Oil Spills. Every day, hundreds of oil spills—some large, others small—occur around the world, usually when crude oil is being stored or transported. Every oil spill affects the environment by spoiling water and land, sending fumes into the air, and harming the plants and animals.

Most crude oil, of course, reaches the refinery without a mishap, but once it gets there, other kinds of pollution take place.

The refining process breaks the crude oil into its chemical components, making gasoline, kerosene, jet fuel, plastics, and hundreds of other products.

After the oil is refined, the products also

have to be transported. And liquid
and gaseous products can be
spilled into the environment just
as crude oil can.

The Good and the Bad. Defi-
nitely, gas and oil have helped
people accomplish great things—
the world would be a very different sort of place to live in today if
these fuels had not been available
to power many important inven-
tions and machines. Gasoline and oil have played a large
part in shaping our lives. Much of their impact has been
good, but the benefits have been costly.

The harmful emissions and the pollution caused by
drilling, transporting, and refining crude oil have caused
illness and even death. The harm done to the environment
can never be fully repaired. Drivers, manufacturers, and oil
companies—all must share the responsibility.

From Start to Finish

Cars cause pollution not only when they are moving but
also before and after their lives on the road.

Producing a car is a complex process. Hundreds of
manufacturing plants and thousands of factories supply
them with parts. Many types of pollution result. The automotive industry is one of the world's major polluters.

New technology has reduced some pollutants in recent
years, but the auto-manufacturing industry around the
world is huge, and most plants still lack pollution controls.

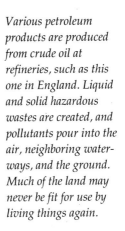

*Various petroleum
products are produced
from crude oil at
refineries, such as this
one in England. Liquid
and solid hazardous
wastes are created, and
pollutants pour into the
air, neighboring water-
ways, and the ground.
Much of the land may
never be fit for use by
living things again.*

Liquid and Solid Wastes. Thousands of gallons of water are used to build a car, mostly for cooling and cleaning the parts that make up the vehicle. Along the way, the water picks up harmful chemicals. Water-treatment plants now clean this water, but at one time it was just dumped into nearby rivers and lakes.

Some manufacturers now use plastics instead of metals for certain parts. This helps, but it still adds some solid wastes to the heap—and more oil is needed to make the plastics.

Air Pollution. Vast amounts of energy are used to make each motor vehicle, and huge amounts of pollution are the result. In the past, most gaseous waste from factories was released into the air. Today, regulations keep this air pollution under control in North America. Special equipment is installed to trap many of the harmful gases and particles.

However, similar improvements have not been made in many auto factories in Mexico, eastern Europe, and some Asian countries. Greater worldwide controls are needed.

The Rusty Finish. Cars have a very limited lifespan—the average car on the road today in the United States is less than eight years old. Most of the cars rolling off the assembly lines by the millions today will be junk within ten years.

And each car that goes to the junkyard will have already sent several tires and batteries there. There are nearly 2 billion tires lying in piles throughout the United States today, and another 250 million are added each year.

Many of the cars are stripped of their useful parts and then crushed, shredded, and recycled to be used again.

But thousands of other cars are just abandoned or left in junkyards, where they slowly rust away. These derelicts are an eyesore, but even worse, they leak fluids containing harmful chemicals. Battery acid, transmission fluid, and motor oil soak into the soil and eventually pollute the groundwater.

There are many processes involved in auto production that can release hazardous materials into the environment. Because of this, the automotive industry is one of the world's major polluters.

The Cleanup Effort

In the United States, the Big Three automakers are all making efforts to clean up their act. Hazardous wastes that were once thrown away carelessly are now carefully controlled and disposed of, or recycled.

Auto manufacturers are working with the oil industry worldwide to reduce the harmful effects of auto emissions and to reduce other forms of pollution as well. Still, these industries continue to rank high as serious polluters. Everyone needs to play a role in finding solutions.

Many experts predict that things will get worse before they get better. Despite the steps being taken to clean the air, motor vehicle emissions are expected to increase about 35 percent by the year 2010. The sheer number of cars will keep things from getting better soon.

Chapter 4

The Promise Broken

IN THE EARLY DAYS of automobiles, advertisements heralded their speedy fun. Cars promised the adventure of the unexplored road, fresh country breezes, and the excitement of the wide-open spaces!

How does this image match today's reality? Do you experience the adventure of the unexplored road? More likely it's the boredom and frustration of the traffic jam.

Fresh country breezes? Try breathing in the choking exhaust fumes of a busy highway.

The wide-open spaces? You're more likely to inch along the road around a car accident.

Automobiles have traveled beyond the exciting promises of yesterday. The sheer number of cars makes it nearly impossible to experience the freedom they once offered.

Benz, Henry Ford, and the rest of those early automakers could never have imagined such problems.

Congestion

In the world's major urban and suburban areas, traffic congestion has become a fact of life. Radio stations warn motorists of traveling times on busy roads, and many commuters spend two or three hours each day crawling along a so-called "expressway," surrounded by thousands of other slow-moving cars.

Cars are supposed to get people around faster, but our reliance on them is slowing us down. Public transportation—trolleys, buses, and subways—once played an important part in moving people throughout the business districts of large cities. But after World War II, many people decided to drive.

The growth in the number of cars worldwide is not expected to slow. More than 100,000 cars roll off the world's assembly lines each day, all adding to the serious traffic congestion found on many roadways.

About this time, suburbs began their incredible growth. People didn't live as close together as they did in the city, so public transportation couldn't operate efficiently. Residents relied on cars to get them around. And as more and more people moved out of the city and away from their jobs, they needed more and more cars to get them back and forth.

The traffic jams caused by all these cars waste thousands of hours of people's time each day—the cost in human productivity amounts to billions of dollars! According to Bruce T. McDowell of the Advisory Commission on Intergovernmental Relations, "If we allow urban and suburban congestion to squeeze the life out of America's cities, we cannot expect to have a healthy and internationally competitive economy."

Building additional highways may seem to be the answer, but officials are finding that new roads are jammed as soon as they are opened. Dr. John Holtzclaw of the Sierra Club confirms this finding: "Massive highway construction will not ease traffic congestion—but will only spread sprawl and congestion to new areas, and increase time lost in congestion, fuel consumption, and smog."

Around 1900, one of the world's top automakers, Mercedes Benz, predicted that the number of cars throughout the planet would one day peak at 1 million. That number was passed only 15 years later. Today, more than 550 million cars roll across the Earth— one car for every ten people.

Since 1970, the number of cars throughout the world has grown by 4.7 percent each year, and the number of buses and trucks has jumped by 5.1 percent yearly. If this trend continues, as most experts predict it will, there will be 1 *billion* vehicles clogging the world's roads by the year 2030.

STOP

Though more roads are being built, highway congestion in the United States continues to worsen. In the next 20 years annual delays in travel time will increase by 5.6 billion hours. The energy used to keep millions of cars idling on U.S. highways will waste an extra 7.3 billion gallons (27.6 billion liters) of fuel per year, according to the Transportation Research Board.

The average driving speed in London, England, where congestion is very high, is only 8 miles (12.9 kilometers) per hour. In Tokyo, Japan, it's even less. On busy California freeways, speeds of 33 miles (53 kilometers) per hour are average, but as the number of cars continues to grow, the average speed is expected to drop to about 15 miles (24 kilometers) per hour by the year 2000.

Emissions

As congestion gets worse, so does the air pollution caused by emissions. Cars spew out more carbon monoxide, nitrogen oxides, and hydrocarbons because the engines work less efficiently at lower speeds. Even more of these pollutants are emitted when cars speed up, slow down, and idle during traffic jams.

Researchers estimate that pollution caused by auto emissions causes 30,000 deaths per year in the United States alone, and the number of people who suffer illness is far higher. A recent Harvard University study shows that people regularly exposed to diesel exhaust fumes may be 42 percent more likely to develop cancer than other people.

In the United States, the National Ambient Air Quality Standards set the amount of ozone, carbon monoxide, and particulates considered safe for humans to breathe. In 1986, between 40 million and 75 million Americans lived in areas that failed to meet these standards.

If the same standards were in place around the world, hundreds of cities couldn't meet them. For example, respiratory diseases due to smog afflict at least 60 percent of the

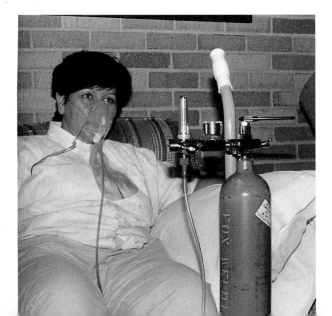

People with respiratory problems, such as this woman who needs additional oxygen, are particularly affected by pollution caused by cars.

residents of Calcutta, India. In Budapest, Hungary, the air's carbon monoxide content is more than twice as high as Hungary's permissible level. And at least six people die each day as a result of smog in Athens, Greece.

Plants in Peril. These pollutants not only affect human health directly, but they also ruin crops. Auto emissions in the United States cause annual yield losses of wheat, corn, soybeans, and beans estimated at $1.9 billion to $4.5 billion, according to the National Crop Loss Assessment Program.

Crop losses will be even greater if global warming is actually taking place, as most scientists think. The changes in temperature around the world would affect growing seasons and climates. The great Wheat Belt in the United States, for example, could become too dry to grow grain. Other regions would have to plant different crops, and humans would simply have to adjust.

Trees—nature's natural air fresheners that put oxygen back into the air—would die because of climate changes, so air pollution would get worse and disease would increase.

Worldwide crop losses due to global warming could be enormous. But even small losses would be devastating to impoverished people living in developing countries, such as this boy in Liberia. Many will starve if their own crops fail.

Acid Rain. Many trees around the world are dying from another problem that cars help create—acid rain, or acid precipitation. The SO_x and NO_x from auto emissions react with moisture in the atmosphere to create acids. These acids fall to the ground in rain or settle on trees and buildings in fog and humidity and soak into the ground when it rains or snows.

Acid rain is blamed for killing forests in many parts of North America and Europe. It spoils lakes and streams along with the plant and animal life within them. Acid rain eats away at statues and buildings, causing great damage.

In Canada, more than 300,000 lakes are in danger of becoming dangerously acidified. Nearly 15,000 are already acidic, and most of the plant and animal life in these lakes is gone.

An Earth Experience

A Close Look at Smog

Smog is a combination of dust, water vapor, and air pollution, including unburned carbon. It forms a dense cloud that may hang over a region for days at a time.

Coat several glass microscope slides with a thin layer of clear petroleum jelly, such as Vaseline. Use another slide to spread the Vaseline into a fine, even film.

Select a variety of sites to place the slides: close to a busy highway, near a factory, in a residential area, and in a rural area. Leave a slide exposed at each location for 24 hours or more. Do not place your slides right after a rainfall, because rain washes many pollutants into the ground. A dry, windy day will produce more dramatic results.

Collect the slides and then study each one under a microscope. With some practice you will be able to sort out specks of carbon, grains of soil, spores, pollen, and other particulates that float in the air. Count the number of each. Draw conclusions as to which site had the greatest pollution. Where was the air cleanest?

In the late 1980s, the Canadian government declared that the country's air pollution must be cut in half by 1994. However, half of the acid rain that affects Canada comes from pollutants spewed out by cars, factories, and power plants in the United States. The acid is carried north on the winds.

The U.S. government has not made a similar commitment to cutting out air pollutants, mainly because the costs to business would be so great. However, recent amendments to the U.S. Clean Air Act will reduce SO_x emissions from coal-burning plants—a big part of Canada's problem.

Forests in many parts of North America and Europe are dying due to acid rain. Exhaust emissions from cars and trucks are a major source of acid rain pollutants.

Safety

Spewing poisonous emissions isn't the only way cars harm and even kill people. Many more people each year are victims of auto accidents. Worldwide, about 250,000 people die each year due to traffic accidents, and 3 million others are seriously injured. That's the equivalent of injuring or killing nearly all the people in the city of Chicago every year!

In the United States, annual traffic deaths hover near the 50,000 mark—far higher than any other country in the world. However, more people are driving more miles in America than anywhere else. If the number of miles per person is averaged out, the death rate among U.S. drivers is comparatively low. There are 2.5 deaths in the United States per 100 million miles (161 million kilometers) traveled, as opposed to 4.2 deaths in France, and 11 deaths in Spain.

Traffic death rates are particularly high in developing countries, where rickety cars share the crowded roads with many pedestrians, carts, bicycles, and animals. According to a World Bank study of 15 developing countries, only intestinal diseases killed more people than traffic accidents.

Safety Belts. One of the best things you can do to stay safe in a car is to wear a safety belt.

In a crash, the car stops abruptly, but everything inside it continues to move at the speed the car was going just before the crash. This is why passengers sometimes fly through the windshield or slam forward into the dashboard. Safety belts hold people in their seats and prevent this from happening. Lap and shoulder safety belts reduce the risk of fatal or serious injuries by 40 to 55 percent.

In the first four years after the state of New York passed a law requiring safety belts, about 10,200 lives were saved and more than 250,000 serious injuries were prevented. New York passed the safety belt law in 1984—the first state to do so—although Puerto Rico, a United States territory, had such a law ten years before.

It's important that safety belts fit well and are adjusted correctly. Shoulder belts should fit snugly and comfortably, while lap belts should fit low across the pelvis, not over the abdomen.

Belts that automatically wrap around the driver or passenger when the ignition is turned on are included in many new cars. These are intended to encourage more people to wear safety belts, but motorists still have to remember to fasten the lap belt for maximum safety. Never let the automatic belt be detached.

Czechoslovakia was the first country to require safety-belt use, in January 1969. The Ivory Coast was second in 1970, followed closely by Japan in 1971, and Australia and New Zealand in 1972.

Among Canadian provinces, Ontario and Quebec took the lead by establishing safety-belt laws in 1976. British Columbia was next, in 1977.

The dummies used in crash tests (left) have one of the toughest jobs in the auto industry, undergoing one crash after another so that researchers can evaluate safety methods. It is especially important that young children always ride in special car seats (right).

School buses are one of the safest forms of motor vehicle transportation, according to the U.S. Department of Transportation. Every day some 350,000 U.S. school buses log approximately 18 million miles (29 million kilometers), safely transporting nearly 22 million students. When crashes occur, injuries are usually minor. Among passengers involved in school bus accidents, 90 percent were either not injured, or received only minor injuries.

FACT

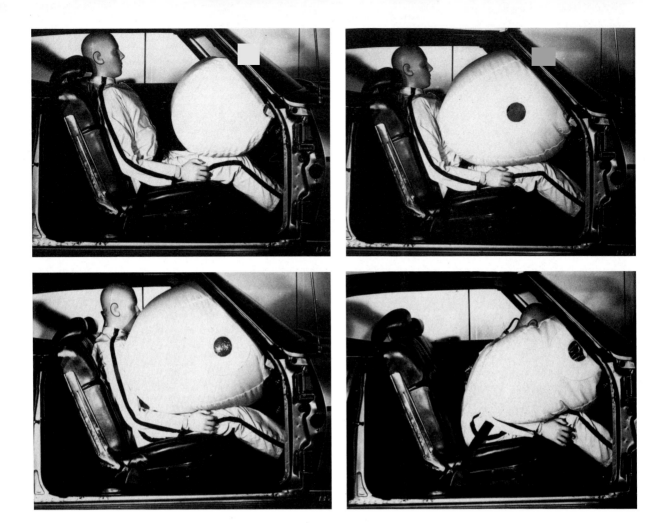

Air Bags. An air bag is like a huge balloon that expands out of the steering wheel or dashboard in front of the car's driver and in front of the passengers, too, in some cars. It provides a cushion that keeps the person from smashing forward. In a crash, sensors on the car signal the air bag to inflate with gas from a quick-acting canister. In about one-twentieth of a second—quicker than you can blink your eye, the bag fills with nitrogen gas. It quickly deflates again to prevent the person suffocating.

An air bag cushions the head and face, while seat belts and shoulder harnesses protect the lower body.

56

Burying the Land with Concrete

As more and more cars are built, people turn over increasingly large parcels of land to motor vehicles. Highways, streets, parking lots, and garages all use nature's land.

Of course, it can be argued that when cars use land, the people in the cars are actually using it. But the vast amounts of space given over to car travel and parking make it valid to question whether there might be better ways of using the limited amount of land on the planet.

In the United States, 60,000 square miles (155,000 square kilometers) of land have been paved over. This is 2 percent of the country's total surface. As much as 10 percent of the country's potential farmland has been used for roadways, at a time when hungry people around the world need food.

There are more than 3.9 million miles (6.3 million kilometers) of streets and highways in the United States. Texas is the state with the most mileage, and California is next.

Much of the world's beautiful landscape is being paved over, so that cars and trucks can get around more easily. There is very little green space left in this section of Orlando, Florida.

In Britain, each mile (1.6 kilometers) of roadway requires 25 acres (10 hectares) of land, and each year up to 4,000 acres (1,619 hectares) of countryside is lost to roads.

Near many crowded cities around the globe, asphalt is

An Earth Experience

Salty Highways

More pollution occurs on many miles of roads when salt—sodium chloride—is applied to them in winter to reduce the freezing point of water. It turns freezing ice and snow into slush, which runs off highways into the soil and neighboring streams, getting into plants. What does salt do to the plant cells?

Obtain some elodea, a common aquarium plant that can be found in a pond or a marsh. It may also be purchased from a pet store. The leaves on this plant are only two cells thick. Remove one of the leaves near the top of the plant. Place it on a slide with a drop of water. Under a microscope, study the streaming cytoplasm and the green bodies containing pigment called chlorophyll. This will give you a picture of what a normal cell should look like.

Put a cover slip over the leaf. With an eye dropper, place a drop of salty water near the edge of the cover slip. Slowly the salty water will seep under and touch the plant cells. The cell walls will not let the salt enter, but instead water is pulled out. (Scientists call this process plasmolysis.*) What does this do to the contents of the cell?*

Salt is great for seasoning food, making cucumbers into pickles, and reducing the growth of bacteria and molds. But when it is used on highways, it kills plant and animal life along the roads. Many cities today are choosing to use sand instead of salt.

covering choice land that could be used to provide adequate homes, parks, and farmland for people. All the dark pavement absorbs heat, causing cities to be hotter than surrounding rural areas. And worldwide, the crisscross of roads through wilderness has cut off rangelands for animals.

Doing Without

Enclosed in our little cocoons of steel, glass, and rubber, we can now travel across vast landscapes without ever breathing in fragrant air or touching grass with our toes. Are we missing something essential?

Of course, while those of us who *have* cars may wistfully wonder if we are missing something, those who don't have cars *know* they are.

It is quite difficult for people who can't afford them to live without cars in a society that runs on car transportation. For people who are too old or too handicapped to drive, transportation can be a nightmare.

People without cars are especially at a loss where mass transportation systems are not readily available. They are the minority in most developed countries, and their needs are often ignored.

Of the 91.6 million households in the United States, autos are owned by 89 percent—81.3 million. Of these households, roughly one-third own one vehicle, another third own two vehicles, and the final third own three or more vehicles. There are about 185 million passenger cars, light trucks, and minivans in the United States.

FACT

Some people can't find jobs because they don't have a car to get them to work. And people who are sick can't get the medical help they need without transportation to doctors and pharmacies. Even when rides can be organized, these people don't have the freedom they could enjoy if they could walk to their destinations.

Still, even though some people don't share in the benefits of cars, all of society is forced to pay at least part of their cost. Study after study has shown that drivers do not pay enough tolls to cover the cost of highways and that taxes on autos and fuel do not cover the real cost of cars.

FACT

The Union of Concerned Scientists estimates that the real cost of gasoline is at least $2.50 per gallon (3.8 liters) more than consumers pay. This cost includes what we must spend for health care and environmental cleanup, productive time lost due to congestion, as well as the cost of maintaining our access to fuel, such as pipelines—and military strength.

Government's Role

It is up to each of us to find solutions to some of these problems on our own. But governments around the world are working to solve other problems by establishing laws and regulations that will help.

In the United States, the Intermodal Surface Transportation Efficiency Act (ISTEA) was passed in late 1991. At a cost of $155 billion over six years, it is expected to help ease many of the problems caused by cars. The act promotes safety by encouraging states to enact mandatory safety belt laws and toughen drunk-driving laws. It also requires auto-makers to provide better safety belts, more air bags, and other safety features on their vehicles.

ISTEA also allows additional money to be spent on highway road construction and maintenance, as well as a federal Scenic Roads program. Unfortunately, only a small portion will be spent on public transportation.

Other governments use different approaches. Several add a high tax to the price of gasoline to make motorists think twice before refilling their tanks. In South Korea, for example, people pay three-and-a-half times as much for gasoline as it costs to import it. The United States is one of only a few countries that import fuel while still keeping taxes low.

The Athens Example. In Greece, the government tried to raise money and limit the number of cars by making people pay a high tax on imported vehicles. However, Greece itself has no auto industry. Many people, in order to avoid the high fee, just make do with their old vehicles. Most of them are poorly tuned gas guzzlers that emit a lot of exhaust fumes. This is one reason that Athens has some of the worst air pollution in the world.

In Athens, they have tried to deal with the pollution situation by using an odd-even scheme to keep cars out of certain areas. Only cars with an even number as the last digit of the license plate can enter restricted areas on even-numbered days, while only odd numbers can enter on odd-numbered days. This method is used in several cities world-wide, with varying degrees of success.

When people follow the rules, it reduces the amount of traffic in the city. However, in Athens and elsewhere, many

Some cities, such as Lyon, France, have banned cars from certain regions for pedestrians to use. Many residents find they enjoy the freedom of walking down car-free streets. And the increasing number of pedestrian shoppers keeps the store owners happy, too.

people cheat. Some, for example, have two license plates, one with an odd final digit and one with an even final digit. In other places, motorists find it easy to break this law by bribing the enforcement officials.

Cars—Keep Out. Some local governments take a more drastic measure—they ban cars from entering the city center. Several different approaches are used, especially in Europe and Indonesia. Sometimes only certain vehicles are allowed into restricted areas, other times no vehicles are allowed on certain days.

In Lübeck, Germany, for example, vibrations and emissions from cars are damaging buildings that date back to the Middle Ages. Cars are now banned from the city center on Saturdays. It may not be a big step, but it is a start.

Creative Car Control. Some governments don't ban cars from any specific areas, but they make it difficult for citizens to own and drive cars.

In Tokyo, for example, anyone wishing to buy a standard-sized vehicle must first show proof that there is a permanent parking space available for the car. To meet this requirement, some homeowners are building garages with elevators that carry their cars to a second-floor parking stall. And in Hong Kong, cars carry a special electronic sensor that records highway travel. Drivers are billed monthly for the amount of time they spent on the road.

The Solution is Willingness

The main burden, though, should not rest on governments to solve the problems caused by cars. Regulations will work only if people support them.

Unfortunately, our love for cars tends to outweigh our desire to solve Earth's problems. Certainly some people are willing to drive smaller cars, but most American consumers want big ones, and automakers keep on making them. Miles of new highways are being paved each day to improve driving conditions. The number of cars worldwide increases each day.

It's clear that people in general have to willingly sacrifice some of their attachment to cars if we want to make positive changes in the environment and in society. Each day that passes without a change in our attitude mires our planet deeper into pollution and land abuse.

Fortunately, there are other methods of fueling cars and getting around that will help make those sacrifices easier.

When drivers must pay fees, called tolls, in order to use highways, they help cover the cost of the road and its upkeep.

Chapter 5

Power with Less Pollution

YOU CHUCKLE AS YOU STEP into your car, thinking back nearly 20 years to the car your family drove in the 1990s. It's hard to believe people actually drove those heavy clunkers that guzzled gallons of gasoline, then spewed it out as clouds of poisonous fumes.

Even then, less damaging cars were available, but hardly anyone drove them. Things sure are better today, in the year 2012. The air is fresh and the sky is blue again. We finally got smart, and now most people drive cars that don't hurt the environment so much.

You're especially proud of your own new car, the shiny Super-Electra EV! This baby is everything the salesman said it would be—a smooth, quiet ride; great acceleration; plenty of power.

You settle in for your journey home after today's business trip. It's a good 250 miles (400 kilometers)—should take you just over four hours at your cruising speed of 60 mph (96 kph). You'll probably stop at a park along the way, though, to refresh yourself. At least you don't have to make those messy stops at gas stations to refuel any more.

The power reserve meter on your dashboard says you've got plenty of power to get home—even some to spare. When you get home, you'll need to plug your car's electric recharging system into the outlet in your garage, but that's simple. Overnight, the car's batteries will be recharged and ready for another long trip tomorrow.

The Future is Here

It all sounds pretty good, doesn't it? Nice cars, easy travel, cleaner air. Well, the technology is available now to

This electric van uses just one of the several types of alternative fuels that can help keep our environment healthier.

make cars like the one we've just been dreaming about. With enough support from governments, industry, and the public, such visions of the future could become reality even sooner.

Electricity is just one of several possible ways to power cars without gasoline. Others are also being tested for future use, as researchers work to design cars that are efficient, economical, and pollution-free.

Certainly, there are obstacles to overcome—plenty of them. Right now, most new types of cars are experimental and built in small numbers. They are costly, and many are unreliable, as were the early gasoline-powered cars. But just as those early cars improved rapidly when the public demanded them, so, too, will the new types of cars improve—if and when the public demands them.

An Earth Experience

Which Cars are Smog Makers?

Cars, trucks, buses, and other gasoline-powered vehicles do not do a good job of completely burning fuel. They release many gases and solid particles into the air. These pollutants are held near the ground level where they go through more than 160 chemical reactions resulting in the hazy, irritating cloud called smog.

Make sure you have adult supervision for this activity. You can run a number of tests to determine what factors affect the amount of solid particles a car gives off. Of course, the most damaging emissions are the gases, but they are much more difficult to capture and measure with a homemade detector.

Construct a holding device for a 4-inch (10-centimeter)-square sheet of white paper. Find a broomstick or a rake handle at least 5 feet (1.5 meters) long. Cut a square of white paper 4 inches (10 centimeters) square and a square of heavy cardboard or wood slightly larger. Tape or nail the larger square to the end of the handle. Spread a thin coat of cooking oil or petroleum jelly on the paper and tack it to the cardboard square.

On a day when there is no wind, ask your parent or another adult to start the car and let it warm up. The engine should idle. Do not race the motor. Standing to the side of the car, extend the stick until the greased paper is about 6 inches (15 centimeters) from the tailpipe. Expose the test paper for one minute. Then shut off the engine and examine the results. Using a magnifying glass, count the number of solid specks in two or three square-inch sections. Calculate an average for one square inch.

Repeat this experiment on a number of vehicles. Perhaps a local car dealer will even let your class test a few brand-new models. Is there a difference in exhausts between a car manufactured in 1980 and one made in 1990 or later? Is a four-cylinder car more efficient than one with eight? Does the fuel used in a car affect the amount of particulates given off? Is regular or premium gasoline better? What about cars or trucks that use diesel fuel? Are some makes of cars better for the environment than others?

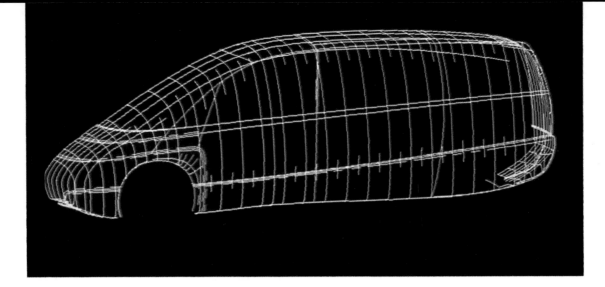

It is important that research, such as computer modeling, be conducted to find healthier, more efficient ways of designing and fueling cars and trucks. Manufacturers and governments must work together, and consumers should demand good results.

The Time Has Come. It is not too soon to begin making these demands. Everyone, including the automobile manufacturers, the oil industry, governments at all levels, and the general public, are aware of the high social and environmental costs of using gasoline and oil as the main fuels for motor vehicles.

A new twist on the internal combustion engine may also prove to be a useful way to conserve fuel. The two-stroke engine uses only two movements of a piston to produce power, as opposed to most engines, which use four strokes. The two-stroke engine is considerably smaller and lighter, making the car more fuel-efficient. However, it releases higher levels of emissions. A two-stroke engine car is being manufactured in Brazil, and Chrysler plans to bring one out in 1996.

According to the United States Department of Energy, it is essential that alternative fuel systems for cars and trucks be developed. Fossil fuels, especially oil, are nonrenewable resources—there is only a limited amount beneath the Earth's surface. Oil will probably run out within the next century—if the pollution from cars and trucks doesn't wipe us out first.

What an Alternative Fuel Needs to Be

In order to be a good replacement for fossil fuels, alternative fuels must meet certain requirements.

Alternative fuels should:

• use renewable resources—resources that people can continue to create.

• be low in cost, so that consumers will be willing to pay for them, and use them in place of fossil fuels.

• be far less damaging to the environment and produce less pollution than gasoline and oil do.

• be safe to handle.

• require few changes in the way cars and trucks look and are driven. People will accept alternative fuels much more quickly if the cars seem familiar and if they are easy to refuel or recharge.

California, Here We Come. Because of the large number of cars and the serious pollution in southern California, people there are paying a good deal of attention to alternative fuels.

The state has ruled that 150,000 vehicles powered by alternative fuels must be produced and on the roads there by

The Doran is one of a few electric cars manufactured by small companies. Electricity is among the most likely fuels to power cars in the future.

1996. By the year 2000, 96 percent of all vehicles sold in the state must have low emission levels. And three years later, at least 10 percent of all new vehicles must make no emissions.

This bus is powered by methanol, a fuel often created from natural gas or coal, or from such renewable resources as wood fiber.

Alternative Fuels Already in Use

Even though vehicles powered by alternative fuels are not widely used by the general public, enough are on the road to prove that the technology works. We may all be driving such cars and trucks someday.

Basically, there are three ways of using alternative fuels in vehicles. *Dedicated use* means that the car or truck will run using only one type of fuel. These are usually the least expensive to build, and they make the most efficient use of fuel. But they are locked into using only one type of fuel and may not be practical if that fuel isn't readily available.

Flexible-fuel vehicles use a mix of more than one fuel at a time. These are more practical and may provide better power, but they are more costly than dedicated use vehicles.

Hybrid-fuel or *dual-fuel* vehicles can switch back and forth between two or more fuels stored on the vehicle. Such vehicles will probably be the next step in cars, since they are quite dependable—if one type of fuel is unavailable, you can switch to another type. They are the most expensive to build but should become cheaper as more people demand them.

A number of different fuels are being used to power these vehicles.

Reformulated Gasoline. This fuel is the obvious choice of the oil companies, since it uses their products and will keep them in business. Though it works in any regular engine just like gasoline, reformulated gasoline has been changed to reduce emissions. Vehicles using reformulated gasoline emit less carbon monoxide and fewer hydrocarbons, though many of the other pollutants remain.

Some of the most-polluted U.S. cities, such as New York, Chicago, Milwaukee, Denver, and Los Angeles, will soon require that reformulated gasoline be burned in vehicles.

A similar development is *oxygenated additives*—liquids that are added to gasoline to increase the amount of oxygen

This flexible-fuel vehicle (right) operates like a regular car, but it runs on a fuel mixture that can vary from 85 percent methanol to 100 percent gasoline. This flexibility allows it to burn a "cleaner" methanol mixture in urban areas and gasoline where methanol is not available. Hybrid-fuel vehicles (bottom), such as General Motor's HX3 prototype, will have the ability to switch between different fuels, such as gasoline and electricity, stored on board.

in the fuel. They help engines in high-altitude cities burn gasoline more efficiently, reducing the carbon monoxide emissions but increasing emissions of formaldehyde, which may cause cancer.

Ethanol. Ethanol has been used as an alternative fuel for a number of years. It is expensive to produce, so it is rarely used as a fuel by itself. Instead, it is often mixed with other fuels.

Ethanol is a grain or corn alcohol. It can also be produced from other grains, plants, farm-field waste, or woods, all of which are known as *biomass* materials. In Brazil, sugarcane is used to produce large quantities of ethanol.

Ethanol is produced from renewable resources, and it cuts down on greenhouse-gas emissions. However, when ethanol is produced from corn, pollution is created by fertilizers and by the machines needed to plant, harvest, and process the corn. Though this pollution can offset the benefits of ethanol, improved agricultural methods can help.

Gasohol—a common ethanol mix—costs about the same as gasoline. It can be used in regular engines without modification. In the United States, gasohol is a mix of 90 percent gasoline and 10 percent ethanol. Gasohol is sold in most states, and some states require that gasohol be made available at gas stations.

Methanol. Methanol, commonly called wood alcohol, is another alcohol fuel. It can be produced from wood fiber, though it is usually made from natural gas or coal. Like ethanol, it's also more practical when blended with gasoline.

Only a limited supply of methanol is available, and

Ethanol can be made from renewable resources in processing plants such as this one, which uses corn to make the fuel.

constructing processing plants is costly—more than $1 billion for each new plant. Methanol might be useful as a possible alternative fuel if gasoline were in short supply. But most methanol is made from nonrenewable resources. The toxic fuel does not significantly reduce pollution, either. If it leaks into water supplies, it can contaminate them.

Soy Diesel Fuel. Soy diesel is a renewable fuel that can replace regular diesel. Made from processed soybean oil, soy diesel can power diesel engines with no modifications, providing the same miles per gallon and power.

It's popular in Europe, where studies show that soy diesel emissions are sulfur-free, particulates and carbon monoxide are greatly reduced, and hydrocarbons are slightly reduced.

At this processing plant in Waterton, Alberta, Canada, natural gas is processed into such fuel components as methane and propane. Bears and other wildlife lost their habitat when this plant was built.

Though soy diesel currently costs about three times as much as regular diesel, its costs will go down if production increases. The fuel is being tested at several locations throughout the United States. In St. Louis, Missouri, for example, several mass-transit buses use soy diesel with good results.

Natural Gas and Propane. Natural gas and propane are two alternative fuels that are readily available throughout most of North America, and they can be used in regular vehicles with fairly minor adjustments to the engines. However, only a few service stations are equipped to handle these fuels.

Natural gas is relatively inexpensive and is available in both liquid and gas forms. Propane, a product of crude oil, is cheap and efficient, but it poses some safety concerns.

Both natural gas and propane are produced from non-renewable resources and present no great benefits in reducing air pollution, although natural gas could help reduce CO and CO_2 emissions. They work best in buses and delivery and service vehicles that can carry the large tanks and are easily maintained.

Electric Vehicles

Electric vehicles (EV) were some of the first cars ever built, but gasoline engines pushed them aside. Now EVs are back, and are considered one of the most likely long-term alternatives to gasoline.

Propane, when used to power a car, must be stored under pressure in large, heavy tanks. These add a good deal of weight to a vehicle, making it less efficient.

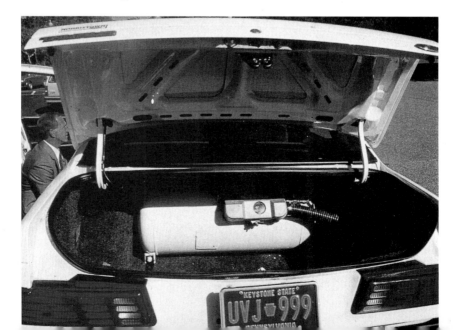

Their electric motors run on power stored in batteries carried on board. The batteries used in most EVs are lead-acid storage batteries. Chemical reaction between the lead, sulfuric acid, and water mixture in the battery creates an electric charge. This electricity flows from the battery to an electric motor, providing the energy to operate the vehicle.

Since no fossil fuels are burned in the engine, EVs have no tailpipe emissions. They are simple to operate, efficient, and quiet. But there are problems too.

After a few hours of operation—currently about 100 miles (160 kilometers)—the car's batteries must be re-charged. This means that an electric current is run into the battery, changing the chemicals back into their original state so they can make an electric charge again. Recharging is accomplished by plugging the car into a regular electric system for six to eight hours—like plugging in a lamp. It's an easy process, but it makes long-distance travel difficult.

The batteries wear out regularly and are heavy, weighing down the car. Most electric motors available now do not provide enough power for quick acceleration or the speed necessary to operate safely in heavy traffic.

The Impact is scheduled for mass production by General Motors in 1994. It will be among the first electric cars built by a large car manufacturer.

For this reason, EVs are best for short trips in light traffic. They may perform nicely for regular commuters who don't travel busy highways, or for business and delivery vehicles that make many brief trips around the city each day.

Electric cars contain batteries (left) that are quite expensive to replace, though they may become less costly as technology improves. They are easily plugged in for recharging (right).

Pollution Problems. Even though they emit no fumes, electric vehicles can cause air pollution in a less direct way. They use electricity, and most of the electricity today is generated by power plants that burn coal or oil. Solar and wind power are being explored as ways to provide pollution-free electric energy.

There is some concern over pollution caused during the manufacture of the batteries, as well as questions over what to do with the batteries once they wear out. The metal and chemicals used in them can create substantial dangers if they are not disposed of carefully. Researchers are looking into ways to recycle most parts.

Many innovative plans and designs must be created before EVs can truly become effective for regular use. All the major car manufacturers, with some government help, have designed plans for an EV—and many have put models on the roads. Also, several small firms are working to develop efficient and inexpensive EVs that look promising for the near future.

According to the United States Department of Energy, the cost of powering an electric vehicle today is approximately twice the cost of powering a similar vehicle with a gasoline engine. This figure must drop drastically if electric vehicles are to become popular.

FACT

Solar Energy

Solar energy is an unlimited and completely renewable source of power. When this energy is converted to electricity to run a car's engine, the vehicle is completely emission-free. There are no tailpipe emissions, and no pollution occurs at the source of the energy—the sun!

Solar-powered vehicles are noise-free and pollution-free, and can be made from nontoxic materials. Solar-powered vehicles don't require motor oil, catalytic converters, or any of the hazardous materials found in gasoline-powered cars, and they can be completely recycled.

Indirect Solar Power. Solar power is used indirectly when energy from the sun is used to create the electricity that powers EVs. This takes place when energy from the sun

The "Pride of Maryland" is a solar car built by students at the University of Maryland for entry in a race featuring solar vehicles.

heats liquids at a solar thermal generating station. Steam from the heated liquid powers a generator, which creates electricity. The electricity generated in this manner is then transmitted to any location where electric vehicles can be plugged in for recharging. So far, generating electricity in this manner is expensive and works well only in areas with lots of sunshine.

Direct Solar Power. Much more interesting and challenging are vehicles that use the sun's power directly. Cars and trucks can be equipped with photovoltaic systems, which produce electricity through the reaction of sunlight on solar cells. Panels of solar cells are mounted on the roof or hood of small, lightweight vehicles. The electricity generated can power the car's electric motor or be stored in batteries.

Vehicles that run strictly on solar energy are still in the experimental stages. Solar power is far more likely to be used on a hybrid vehicle, which will rely on electric batteries or some other fuel for additional power.

Annual competitions among students from various universities are held to increase interest in solar-powered vehicles. Unfortunately, the United States government quit funding research into solar power in the 1980s.

SOLAR-POWERED CAR

1. *Solar Panels* (photovoltaic cells) convert sunlight to electricity.

2. *Computer* decides whether to store electricity in the battery or send it on to the motor.

3. *Batteries* store electricity in the battery or send it on to the motor.

4. *Motor Controller* sends electricity smoothly and efficiently to the motor as needed, controlled by a normal "gas pedal."

5. *Motor* — Electricity magnetizes a coil of wire and forces it to spin.

6. *Drive Train* — The motor turns wheels with a single belt or chain.

7. *Grid Connection* — Most electric vehicles plug into the electric power grid to extend their range.

Fuels for the Future

Though solar power isn't likely to become a regular source of alternative fuel for a number of years, some power sources are even more futuristic. Though working samples exist, a good deal of research and development needs to be done to make both hydrogen and fuel cells into effective alternative fuels.

Hydrogen. Hydrogen could be one of the most ideal alternative fuels. When it is made from water, hydrogen is a renewable resource. When it is used in an automobile, there are no tailpipe emissions, other than a small amount of nitrogen compounds and water vapor.

The hydrogen used as fuel is often made by electrolysis, in which water molecules are split into hydrogen and oxygen. Little pollution is caused, but this method is costly. Hydrogen can also be produced from fossil fuels. This is less costly, but a lot of pollution is created in the process.

Pure hydrogen can be stored in either liquid or gaseous form, and either way, it is difficult to store and transport. Liquid hydrogen must be stored and shipped at the extremely low temperature of -425 degrees F. (-220 degrees C), and hydrogen gas must be stored under very high pressure. Sometimes hydrogen is stored in compounds called metal hydrides. Research is underway to store hydrogen on carbon granules, which are light and compact.

Fuel Cells. Somewhat like a battery, a fuel cell combines hydrogen and oxygen, which react to form water, giving off a large amount of electricity in the process. This electricity can be used to power vehicles. Though fuel cells are expensive, large, and heavy, they are still very efficient.

Fuel cells give off very few pollutants. It would take 1,600 engines powered by fuel cells to produce gases equal to the

The LaserCel™ (above), a hydrogen fuel cell, utilizes the safest hydrogen fuel storage available. Hydrogen is stored in a metal hydride powder. When used as a fuel, hydrogen's primary emission is water, which makes it the ideal, environmentally safe fuel. Mazda's HR-X (below), a hydrogen-fueled car, is being developed for use in the 21st century.

exhaust emissions of just one internal combustion engine powered by gasoline.

Fuel cells have been used in the space shuttles and on the moon to power exploration vehicles (moonbuggies), but they are currently impractical for use in cars on Earth.

It will take several years to develop fuel cells that are small and inexpensive enough for general use in vehicles. And since extremely high temperatures are generated by some types of fuel cells, safety problems must also be overcome. But fuel cells may be an ideal source of energy to power vehicles in twenty years or so.

What Happens Next?

No single alternative way of fueling a car clearly stands out as the best. Each has its advantages and disadvantages. They must all continue to be tested carefully.

Certain fuels are more beneficial and effective in specific geographic areas, such as ethanol's use in the Midwest, where corn is plentiful. Low-emission fuels, such as electricity, can be developed most effectively in California, where there is a great need for such fuels. Solar power is most promising in regions with lots of sunshine. Each area can play a role in testing and developing specific energy sources.

In the long run, both hydrogen and fuel cells offer many advantages, but many billions of dollars must be spent on research and development. Only strong support and regulations by state and federal governments will keep research and development alive. The public must demand more efficient cars with less pollution. And we must be willing to pay the price for them if our Earth is to be habitable during the next century.

Chapter 6

Have You Ridden a Bike Lately?

TWO CITIES IN A STATE renowned for its love of the automobile are proving something to the rest of the United States. Davis and Palo Alto, both college cities in California, are persuading some of their citizens to give up their cars. Many use bicycles instead.

In Davis, a town of 44,000, 25 percent of all trips—to the store, to work, or to school—are made by bike. More than a quarter of the city's roads have bicycle lanes, and there are about 17 miles (32 kilometers) of bike paths.

Palo Alto also has plenty of bike riders. About $1 million in state grants paid for projects to promote cycling. Bike bridges and lighted paths make biking more convenient, as do the bike lockers and racks installed in many locations. In addition, new business buildings must provide a place for employees to park their bikes—and even a place for them to shower after riding to work.

Unfortunately, Davis and Palo Alto are unusual. Cars are by far the main form of transportation in most communities throughout North America. But the success of the two California cities in cutting down on car traffic proves that drivers are willing to use other methods to get around, if those methods are convenient.

Many bicyclists enjoy the trails around Davis, California, and use them for commuting as well as pleasure.

Beyond Convenience. Admittedly, it's hard to beat cars for convenience. Few other forms of transportation get you directly from your home to your destination. But people have to realize that there is more than just convenience at stake. As you know, the hazards caused by cars are putting people, and even our planet, at risk!

And as the number of cars continues to increase, jamming roadways and slowing average speeds to a turtle's pace, perhaps even cars aren't so convenient anymore. For many people, a daily commute of two hours or more in their cars is a part of life. But more and more people are beginning to feel that it's a terrible waste of time—and it is ruining the quality of their lives.

It's time to consider other forms of transportation that are healthier for us and for our world.

Bicycles

Bicycles were invented in the early 1800s, and they've been popular ever since. In fact, bicycles are the most common form of transportation around the world—they outnumber cars two to one. In many countries, people use bikes to get to work and other important destinations.

Among Europeans, the greatest numbers of bike riders are found in small, compact countries, such as Denmark and the Netherlands. There, nearly one-third of all trips made within cities are made by bicycle.

Bicycling in the United States. In the United States, however, bikes are used mainly for recreation. Of the approximately 90 million bikes in the United States, less than 3 million carry their owners to work regularly.

More than half the trips people make to work in the United States are about 4.5 miles (7.2 kilometers) or less. That's an easy distance to ride a bike. Those who travel longer distances might ride their bikes to the train or bus station. Bike riders can often get around more quickly than drivers, too, especially in busy urban areas where the crush of traffic congestion slows cars to a crawl.

In Asia, bicycles often make up two-thirds of the vehicles in city streets during rush hours. In China, there are 300 million bicycles and only 1.2 million cars.

The average American commuter who gets to public transportation by bicycle rather than by car will save approximately 150 gallons (576 liters) of gasoline each year. The average American who drives all the way to work can save 400 gallons (1,514 liters) of gas each year by switching to bicycling and mass transit.

Bicycling is a great form of healthy transportation. It's clean for the environment, good exercise, and fun too!

Solving Problems. Bicycles add no harmful emissions to the atmosphere, they consume no fossil fuels, and few resources are used in their production. Also, bikes require less land to be set aside for travel and parking than cars do.

Some communities are making it easier for cyclists to get around by installing bike lanes along busy roadways, and by making sure that all roads and bridges are open to bikes, that repairs are smooth and easy to cycle over, and that bike racks and bike-parking areas are available.

Biking Benefits. Many things can be done to make biking more convenient. It's a great form of transportation—one that deserves more consideration.

Marcia Lowe of the Worldwatch Institute has said, "The bicycle is the only vehicle that can address all the problems we've inflicted on ourselves, such as air pollution and congestion in our cities, and still give us an individualized way of getting around."

Ride-Sharing

When two or more people share a ride to work or school and back on a regular basis, it is called car pooling. Because car poolers aren't all driving separate cars, there are fewer cars on the road. Something as simple as that is a start toward cleaning the environment.

Car pooling became popular during World War II, when

the United States needed as much fuel as possible to power tanks and trucks. It was considered un-American to waste gasoline. A popular public service advertisement at the time encouraged motorists to "Join a Car-Sharing Club Today," adding, "When you ride ALONE you ride with Hitler!"

Currently, U.S. motorists waste a total of 2 billion hours each year sitting in urban traffic. U.S. highway officials estimate that over the next 20 years, traffic congestion will increase by more than 400 percent on the freeways and 200 percent on other roads.

FACT

Today, car pooling is usually an informal arrangement between people who work and live near each other. Some businesses help coordinate car pools for their employees.

Sometimes, one person drives all the time and the other riders pitch in with money to cover expenses. Other times, members of the car pool take turns driving their cars.

Van Pooling. A number of people sharing a ride in a vehicle larger than a car is called van pooling. The practice began during the early 1970s when gasoline was expensive and in short supply. It still remains a good way to cut down the number of cars on the highway.

Sometimes the van is owned by the driver, and other passengers help share expenses. Businesses may purchase vans for groups of employees to use. In some cases, an outside firm—such as the local public transit agency—owns the vans. One of the people in the van pool is chosen as the driver and is paid a small amount for that task. The rest pay a regular fee to ride in the van.

An Earth Experience

Car Pooling, or One-in-One

You can find out how much car pooling goes on in your community. It won't be a very scientific survey, but it may give you a rough idea of what is happening. The next time you and your family go on a trip, even just to a nearby town, count the number of people in each car you see. (If you live on a busy highway, you can do this activity sitting in your front yard.)

If you do this study in a car, be sure you are sitting in the back on the driver's side with a clear view of the traffic. Ask another family member or a friend to record the numbers while you call them out. You will need to keep your eyes on the oncoming cars so you don't miss one.

The best time to conduct this activity is during the morning or late afternoon when most people are going to work or returning from their jobs. Repeat the count on a weekend. Repeat the survey several times in different directions on trips out of town. If there is a difference, can you offer some reason for it? What is the highest number of people you counted in any one car? Did the group look like a family or a car pool?

What conclusions can you draw from your results? Will pollution be relieved by car pooling? Could people in your community be doing more toward these goals?

Pooling Pluses. Car pooling and van pooling have a lot of benefits for the riders—pooling is cheaper and less stressful than driving and it allows passengers to read or relax as they ride. The benefits to the environment are even greater. Ride-sharing eases some of the congestion that chokes busy freeways. It also conserves fuel and reduces pollution.

In high-traffic areas around the world, governments often encourage ride-sharing by having special highway lanes that can be used only by vehicles carrying at least two—sometimes three or four—people. Often called HOV lanes (short for high-occupancy vehicle lanes), these special lanes save commuters lots of time.

During an average rush hour on a four-lane freeway, three lanes may be clogged with standstill traffic while cars in HOV lanes whiz by smoothly. This advantage rewards those who share rides and encourages people stuck in traffic to consider joining a pool themselves!

One special highway lane for buses and other shared-ride vehicles handles the same number of commuters as three regular lanes, according to the American Public Transit

Several cities use education posters to convince commuters to use ride-sharing and mass transit systems to ease traffic congestion.

Association. Such pooling thus eliminates the need to widen roads, which would cover over more land.

Public Transportation

Public transportation in North America started in the mid-1800s, at a time when cities and industrial centers were growing rapidly. Street railways, like small trains with rails mounted in the pavement, carried people from residential into business areas. They were powered first by horses and then, around the turn of the century, by electricity. These were the first light-rail systems. Some new systems are being built today.

These railways, the main form of transportation in big cities at that time, could barely keep up with the demand. In some areas, elevated railways built above streets noisily picked up the slack. And in 1897 in Boston, another new form of transportation appeared on the scene—the underground subway. The New York subway opened in 1904.

As cities and national prosperity grew, so did mass-transit systems. But after World War I, the popularity of cars changed the way people got around. More people drove themselves—fewer took public transportation. However, in the congested central business districts of large cities, people continued to use the transit systems.

The Great Depression of the 1930s and World War II in the 1940s left money tight throughout the country, so people once again turned to public transportation. But when the economy improved, ridership shrank.

About this time, something else was taking place that would change the shape of public transportation in the United States. Beginning in the 1930s, General Motors joined forces with other businesses to buy more than 100 electric-rail systems in 45 cities. They dismantled them and paved over the tracks, so that more people would be required to purchase and drive cars or to ride buses—also made by General Motors. By the late 1950s, nearly 90 percent of the country's electric light-rail network was gone.

But the buses that replaced streetcars and trolleys in many areas were inadequate. In the suburbs, where people didn't live very close together, there was no way to make public transportation run effectively and make a profit. It looked like the end of public transit throughout the country.

But it wasn't. Government officials felt that public transit was too important to let die, so in the early 1970s, the government took over, using tax dollars to support the mass-transit systems. The new investment of money was used to spruce up old buses and subway cars, to expand the system so that more people could use it, and to increase ridership by advertising to attract more riders. Today, local and federal governments are spending millions of dollars to rebuild transit systems.

For every average American who quits driving a car to work and instead rides a bus, air pollution annually is reduced by 9 pounds (4.1 kilograms) of hydrocarbons, 63 pounds (28.6 kilograms) of carbon monoxide, 5 pounds (2.3 kilograms) of nitrogen oxide, and 1 pound (0.4 kilogram) of particulates. About 10 to 15 gallons (38 to 57 liters) of gasoline are saved every time a full load of 40 people takes a 10-mile (16-kilometer) trip to work on a bus, rather than in individual cars.

Buses. Bus service is by far the most common type of public transportation in the United States. Though most buses run on fossil fuels, adding pollutants to the air, the amount is less than if all the bus passengers drove separately in their own cars.

Each commuter who travels by bus cuts hydrocarbon emissions by 90 percent and carbon monoxide emissions are cut by more than 75 percent over those given off by a private car. Nitrogen oxide and particulate emissions are reduced between 10 and 15 percent.

Bus lines are a flexible type of service, since drivers can easily add a route in a growing area or cut out service to a region where businesses have closed. Buses can make as many or as few stops along their runs as necessary, depending on the time of day.

This flexibility is what makes buses popular, but it is also a drawback. Frequent stops to pick up and drop off passengers slow down their progress. And buses get stuck in traffic jams just as cars do. Where HOV lanes are available, however, buses are more reliable.

More people ride buses (left) *than use any other type of public transportation in North America. Elevated trains run on rails built over the street* (right), *such as the San Francisco Bay Area Rapid Transit (BART). Many commuters throughout the metropolitan area use BART each day.*

Personal Rapid Transit. Small cars running on elevated tracks make up the basis for personal rapid transit systems. A car, guided by computer programs, arrives at a stop when summoned by a rider. Each car carries up to three passengers to a destination they program in. No driver is required.

Still a very new idea, personal rapid transit systems are being tested in a few cities around the world. So far they have proven to be efficient. Though the costs of building the system are high, the actual operating costs are quite low.

Personal rapid transit systems, such as the one shown below, are being developed. They offer riders the ability to go to specific destinations.

Rail Systems. Rail systems can be broken down into several categories.

Light-rail transit includes street-cars and trolleys, in which rail cars run independently on rails. These systems are quite popular where they exist, and more are being built in a number of cities including San Diego and Sacramento.

Heavy-rail systems, also known as rapid transit, are much more

common. These include subways, surface trains, elevated trains, and commuter railways, which run from central urban areas to suburbs and rural regions. Most large cities throughout the world use a combination of heavy-rail systems, in addition to buses, for public transportation.

Moscow's rapid transit system is the busiest in the world, followed by Tokyo, Paris, New York City, and London.

Passenger Trains. When American passenger trains went out of business about 1970, the federal government formed a system called Amtrak, the only railroad that crosses the country. However, Amtrak's lines run mainly in the northeastern states, where people depend heavily on trains.

Though Amtrak doesn't reduce commuter traffic, it does give people an alternative to driving or flying long distances, thus easing highway congestion in and around airports.

In Canada, there is no longer a cross-country passenger-train system—the last one was shut down in the late 1980s due to the dwindling number of passengers.

Throughout North America, freight train systems, too, are dying, even though trains are four times as fuel-efficient as trucks at hauling freight. Tracks and rail cars are falling into disrepair, and business is slowing down, since trains haul shipments to only a few locations, where the freight still has to be picked up by trucks. Giant semi-trailer trucks, however, can take loads directly to their destinations. The number of trucks on the road is growing to meet the demand.

High-Speed Trains. High-speed train service is a relatively new type of mass transit. These trains travel at speeds of 100 to 300 mph (160 to 480 kph), making it convenient for commuters to travel between fairly close cities regularly.

The number of high-speed trains is growing in the United States, where Amtrak is helping states to develop their own systems. The Metroliner, for example, reaches 125 mph (200 kph) on its regular run between New York City and Washington, D.C. More such systems are being planned between major cities in Texas and in Ohio.

Magnetic-levitation trains, often called maglevs, are another type of high-speed train attracting interest around the world. Powerful electromagnets in tracks raise rail cars up about 6 inches (15 centimeters) and carry them along at speeds of up to 300 mph (483 kph). Maglevs have been tested in Germany and Japan.

Maglevs emit only one-fourth as much carbon dioxide as airplanes and reduce other pollutants as well. But they also create noise pollution and are much more expensive than high speed trains.

Mass Transit Advantages. When two or more passengers ride together in a vehicle, a step is taken to help improve the quality of air and reduce traffic congestion.

The most famous high-speed train is Japan's "Bullet Train" (Shinkansen), *which travels between Tokyo and Osaka at an average speed of 130 mph (210 kph).*

In most cars on the road, the national average passenger load is 1.2 persons during commuting times. Compare that to the typical bus, which carries an average of 17 passengers, and the subway car, which carries an average of 37.

In some cities, average loads are even higher, making an even greater contribution to air quality. In Chicago, for example, 80 percent of the 2 million commuter trips to and from the central business district are made on mass transit.

Riding on rail systems rather than in a car greatly reduces harmful emissions. The pollution emissions for electrically powered rail services such as subways and light-rail lines are measured from the power plants that generate the electricity to move the vehicles.

Hydrocarbons and carbon monoxide emissions are reduced by more than 99 percent when the average commuter rides either heavy rail or light rail instead of driving a car. In addition, nitrogen oxide emissions are reduced by more than 60 percent, and particulate emissions decrease by more than 90 percent.

Funding Mass Transit. Mass transportation systems are supported by taxpayers, but some people believe that federal, state, and local governments should do more. They believe that less money should be spent on road improvements and expansions and more to increase the use of mass transit systems.

"Mass transit is something positive government can do to protect air quality, conserve energy, promote desirable land-use patterns, and provide access to jobs and convenient, safe travel," according to Joanne R. Denworth, of the Pennsylvania Environmental Council in Philadelphia. "It's hard to think of a government spending program where so much bang can be gotten for the buck."

Federal funds for public transportation shrank from $4.6 billion in 1981 to $3.7 billion in 1992. Currently, the federal government provides only about 20 percent of all funding for public transit—10 years ago it gave about 40 percent.

Fortunately, state and local governments have picked up the slack, and the total amount of public funding for mass transportation systems has actually risen.

Urban Planning

Half as many Americans walked to work in 1990 as in 1960, and, also, half as many people ride public transportation, according to the Eno Foundation for Transportation. People's dependence on cars could be reduced by careful urban planning. If homes were built nearer stores, offices, and factories, residents could walk to their jobs, and do their shopping on foot.

In Los Angeles, where residents rely on their cars to carry them through the city's vast sprawl, planners recently determined that highway building and mass transit would not be enough to solve the city's monumental traffic problems. Instead, they determined, people simply need to live closer

In order to decrease our dependence on cars, urban areas need to be compact, with affordable housing. Many European cities have set an example, with good mass-transit systems in residential areas.

97

to where they work and shop, so that traffic can be cut.

Unfortunately, the cost of housing near jobs in the urban centers of Los Angeles and other large cities is well beyond the reach of most people.

In Washington, D.C., planners are making an effort to build most of the city's new shopping, office, and residential developments within easy walking distance of subway stops, and bus lines and Amtrak.

Toronto's Transit. It's easiest, of course, to reduce dependence on cars in new communities that are specially designed for this. But several established cities in Canada, including Toronto, have done quite well at cutting down on car travel, proving that it can be done in other places. Forty percent of commuters in Toronto use mass transit.

In Toronto, developers have been encouraged to build their projects in specific locations near subway stops. Growth has been limited in the city center, while new rail lines encourage people moving to the city's outer edges to use mass transit. City planners throughout the rest of the world need to study Toronto's example.

Telecommuting. New technology has opened up another option that may allow many people to cut back on their commutes to work—telecommuting. Through the use of computers and telephones, employees can hook into their offices and share information and ideas with co-workers, all from home. Many people could eliminate several trips to the office each week this way.

Another version of telecommuting consists of college and adult education classes being broadcast on television, so that students can watch from their homes instead of at school.

Both these forms of telecommuting are rapidly gaining in popularity. People enjoy the comfort, ease, and flexibility of staying home while getting their work done. It's a great bonus that pollution is cut down, since all their cars stay at home!

Options Needed

It's clear that there are many ways to reduce car use around the world. Perhaps the best approach is to make many options available, so that people can use the method of transportation that works best for them.

Florida is setting a good example. Officials are working to meet the expanding transportation needs in this fast-growing state. Developers must show that local roadways and transit systems can handle the number of people who will live or work in the buildings or developments they are putting up. Many businesses provide car pools, van pools, and shuttle buses for their employees. And the state government is planning to build a high-speed rail system to carry people long distances within the state.

Most people are willing to try other options—if they are available and affordable—instead of always driving. Governments, through careful planning, need to make sure that car travel is safe for people and the planet, and they must also provide alternative means of public transportation.

According to the Worldwatch Institute, half of all apartments built in Toronto since 1954 are within walking distance of rapid rail transport, and nearly 90 percent of all new offices are built next to rail stations. Some major business developments have subway stations underneath them.

Chapter 7

The Final Challenge

CAN YOU IMAGINE GOING TO your favorite fast-food restaurant and ordering a meal of sautéed liver, steamed broccoli, and carrot juice?

It probably won't happen, will it? And why not? You know these things are healthy—certainly better than a cheeseburger, fries, and a strawberry shake. But if you're like most people, you don't always want what's good for you. You want what you like—what you are familiar and comfortable with.

That's sort of how it is with cars. Most people today realize that cars are hurting our world, but they still want to drive them. They want gasoline-powered cars, because that's what they've always driven, and they want them big and fast, because that's fun and convenient.

So what the public wants, the public gets. That's how business works in what is called a "market-driven" economy. Businesses produce goods that meet the needs and desires of their customers. The auto industry is simply responding to demand. Why should they build safer, more efficient vehicles, or cars that run on alternative fuels, if no one wants to buy them?

Of course, the auto industry has a responsibility to educate buyers about the benefits of these different sorts of vehicles. And certainly they should try harder to make these vehicles more attractive to buyers.

But a big share of the responsibility lies with us—the consumers. If and when we decide that we want vehicles that are better for our health and the health of our planet, the industry will respond and make such vehicles available.

And if we demand better public transportation, or more

environmentally sound ways of disposing of old cars, businesses will make them available, too.

The best way to achieve good results in any major project is by working together. If the automotive industry, the government, and the public cooperate to solve the problems posed by cars, the Earth will be a healthier place.

Automobile Manufacturers

Cars and trucks produced before 1970 were extremely heavy polluters. They burned leaded gasoline and had few emissions controls. For a while, the automobile manufacturers were unaware of the environmental damage caused by cars, and then they ignored it.

However, when the United States government passed the Clean Air Act of 1970, the exhaust emissions of new cars were reduced. Hydrocarbons and carbon monoxide have been cut by 96 percent and nitrogen oxides by 76 percent. In the 1960s, the average car got about 14 mpg (6 kpl). By the early 1990s, the average new car could go twice as far on a gallon of gas. Current regulations penalize car makers when the entire fleet of cars they produce each year averages less than 27.5 mpg (11.7 kpl).

The automotive industry is spending billions of dollars to respond to other environmental concerns as well. Their manufacturing facilities and processes are being cleaned up and improved. Research to reduce the environmental damage caused by cars and trucks is being done. And test vehicles using alternative fuels are being produced and studied.

Carmakers are responding to the challenge, but they are not doing enough. Every year, there are more cars on the road and more miles traveled. So even though some im-

Emissions tests are performed on all new models of automobiles to determine the amount of pollutants spewed out by cars.

provements have been made, problems are still increasing.

Gas consumption, for example, could be reduced if all available technology were used. Car manufacturers have the know-how to produce cars that get 70 mpg (29.8 kpl).

But there is a lack of public demand, so only small numbers of fuel-efficient cars are being produced. Manufacturers complain that these cars cannot be produced at a profit. On the other hand, the small trucks, vans, and medium- and large-sized passenger cars demanded by the public are being turned out in dozens of models, loaded with options that increase their price while decreasing their efficiency.

The Oil Industry

Following World War II, the oil industry in North America grew rapidly, along with the auto industry. A large supply of foreign oil was available, and the amount of oil found in the United States was plentiful, too.

Exploration and drilling for new oil was going on in many places with little regard for the environment. Lots of damage was done to the Earth, but the companies grew wealthy, and little thought was given to the planet.

But the Arab oil embargo of 1973 shook up the oil industry, as well as consumers. The nation's dependence on for-

eign oil suddenly became painfully obvious. Even more
drilling operations were started within the United States.

At the same time, many industries and power plants
began to seek out other sources of power. Coal and nuclear
power were two replacements. But the transportation industry did little to find alternative energy sources. Gasoline and
diesel were still tops for cars.

Auto manufacturers worked to conserve oil by building
smaller cars that used less fuel, but shortly after the oil
embargo ended, manufacturers and consumers returned to
their favorite big, heavy cars in large numbers.

To its credit, the oil industry has made an effort to reduce
some of the pollutants in fuel. Lead additives are no longer
used. Research continues to develop cleaner and more efficient ways to use gasoline and oil in cars, but the basic
chemical makeup of these fuels means that they will always
emit harmful fumes when they are burned, so gasoline
engines will always produce tailpipe emissions.

The industry has not shown much interest in developing
other types of fuels either. But alternative fuels must replace
gasoline and oil in vehicles in coming decades.

The Recycling Industry

Steps must also be taken to keep old cars and their parts
from taking up precious space on the planet as they slowly
rust and rot away. Recycling is the answer, and it is up to
businesses and car owners to cooperate and do their parts.

A good example of such cooperation took place recently
in California. Unocal, one of the country's largest oil companies, sponsored a program called the South Coast Recycled
Auto Project (SCRAP) to help clean up the air around Los
Angeles—the worst in the nation.

At least 60 percent of the region's air pollutants come
from cars and other motor vehicles, and it is the older cars,
built before air-quality standards took effect in the 1970s,
that do the most damage. So the SCRAP program set out to
purchase 7,000 autos built before 1971. They paid $700 for
each and recycled them all. Contributions allowed them to
purchase and recycle 8,376
vehicles.

*A good deal of pollution
can be prevented and oil
can be conserved if
motor oil is recycled.
This tank truck is
collecting used oil for
recycling.*

Most of the cars purchased
under SCRAP were big, old
American cars. Many were
tested before being processed,
and researchers found that the
cars' emissions were actually
twice as "dirty" as expected.

As much as 75 percent (by weight) of the materials used in the average car on the road is recyclable, though far less than that is actually recycled. The steel, aluminum, and iron in cars are reused the most.

Recycle that Wreck. Many different parts of a car can be reused. Sometimes, the metal parts are smelted and the material is formed into some other object. The same holds true for plastics. Volkswagen, for example, is the first car manufacturer to use recycled plastic from other car bumpers on its own bumpers. These are found on the VW Polo cars.

The lead-acid batteries used in cars for ignition and lighting are also easily recyclable. It is illegal to throw lead-acid batteries in the trash—the lead and acid in them can be very harmful to the environment if not handled properly.

FACT

The U.S. Environmental Protection Agency estimates that 80 percent of all lead-acid batteries are now being recycled. This recycling rate is even greater than the rate for aluminum cans and five times greater than the rate for glass bottles.

Car owners can take their dead batteries to battery dealers or service stations, where they are collected and then delivered to a lead-recycling facility. There, the batteries are separated into their component parts, which are recycled.

Some communities are helping to make it easier for car

owners to recycle their batteries. Milwaukee, Wisconsin, for example, has drop-off centers where the batteries are collected for recycling. In Reading, Pennsylvania, some garbage trucks are equipped with compartments to carry batteries.

Tired Tires. Used tires create special problems. In Canada, more than 26 million car tires are discarded each year. Many municipal landfills will not accept them. The costs in terms of landfill space are excessive. The Minister of the Environment is trying to improve the situation, by encouraging use of scrap tire rubber in products and by promoting recycling.

Americans discard about 250 million tires each year. However, tires can be turned into fuel and other useful products. Each tire can produce 1 gallon (3.8 liters) of oil; gas equal in heating value to 60 cubic feet (1.7 cubic meters) of natural gas; coke equal to 7 pounds (3.2 kilograms) of coal; and 1 pound (0.45 kilogram) of steel. In addition, the heat created to process the tires can be recovered and used to produce hot water, steam, or electricity.

About 2 billion scrap tires are stockpiled throughout the United States right now. Somewhere between 70 to 85 percent of all scrapped tires are left in landfills and stockpiles, where they create fire and health hazards. However, there are ways to reuse tires.

A fire on a huge lot holding discarded tires sent forth poisonous smoke over Hagersville, Ontario, Canada, in 1990 (left). The soil and groundwater were also polluted. Similar disasters can be avoided if more tires are sent to be deliberately incinerated for energy production (right).

Used tires—either the whole tires or tire-derived fuel—are burned for energy by cement kilns, pulp and paper mills, utilities, and specialized tire-to-energy facilities. About 8 to 11 percent of all scrapped tires are used in this way. It is expensive to start up such an operation, though, and modifications need to be made to exhaust systems in order to meet air-quality requirements. In addition, there is the risk that the tire supply might dwindle, and the fuel would no longer be readily available.

Scrap tire rubber can also be used in asphalt paving, either as part of the binding material or as seal coat. It takes about 1,600 recycled tires to provide rubber seal coat for each mile (1.6 kilometers) of two-lane road.

However, high initial costs keep this material from being used on many roadways. In addition, another scrap material—polyethylene—also works well and since it costs less, it will probably be the material of choice in most paving operations. Only about half of 1 percent of all scrapped tires are used in paving.

What's Left Over. One of the biggest problems associated with auto recycling, though, is what to do with the materials that can't be used again.

"Shredder waste" is the material that remains after cars have been processed for recycling and the metal and plastic have been removed. Since it contains dangerous levels of lead and other heavy metals, shredder waste is considered hazardous waste, and it must be handled carefully.

If parts such as batteries and exhaust pipes are removed prior to shredding, the toxic levels are greatly reduced, and shredder waste can be disposed of in landfills not specifically designed for hazardous waste. Still, the need for landfill space to hold shredder waste is growing.

Government Involvement

When a problem becomes serious enough, government often steps in to create laws that will benefit citizens. Safety belts are a good example. Cars have been equipped with them for several decades, but few people used them until laws were passed requiring people to wear safety belts.

Perhaps the government should step in and make laws about healthier cars, too. The government could require that only certain kinds of cars be sold. Some regulations like that are already in place.

At the nationwide level, the U.S. Clean Air Act of 1970 and its revisions are examples of laws passed to help the citizens. However, the U.S. Congress and president have done little to solve other environmental and safety concerns involving motor vehicles and transportation.

At the Government Level, What Can be Done? Many actions can be taken by all levels of government. Deborah Gordon with the Union of Concerned Scientists, in her book *Steering a New Course*, offers several suggestions.

The federal government could:

1. Raise the fuel economy requirement for average passenger cars from 27.5 mpg (11.7 kpl) to 40 mpg (17 kpl) or more by the year 2000.

2. Raise fuel taxes across the board, and add taxes to gas-guzzling cars.

3. Establish and enforce lower speed limits on highways.

4. Encourage and fund mass transit and HOV.

5. Provide funding for research and development of clean, alternative fuels and fuel systems.

6. Establish taxes on cars with heavy tailpipe emissions.

7. Support a strong cross-country rail network, perhaps by expanding Amtrak.

8. Tax heavy trucks.

9. Support research and development of non-polluting forms of energy.

The state and provincial governments could:

1. Make sure government-owned vehicles are fuel-efficient and have few tailpipe emissions.

2. Raise state fuel taxes.

3. Offer incentives for purchase of fuel-efficient and low-pollution vehicles.

4. Lower and enforce speed limits.

5. Adapt strict pollution-control policies similar to those in California.

6. Establish user fees for all types of transportation within the state or province.

7. Encourage alternative transportation, such as ride-sharing, bicycling, and walking.

8. Work with the federal government in the development and use of clean, alternative fuels.

At the local level:

1. Support and encourage the use of mass transit.

2. Encourage park-and-ride and similar programs.

3. Provide better pedestrian and bicycling facilities.

4. Penalize drivers who carry no passengers.

5. Raise parking fees.

6. Sponsor education programs.

7. Coordinate transportation and land-use planning.

Local, state, and federal governments need to take leadership roles in establishing priorities and programs that encourage more efficient ways of using cars and mass transit.

We have all enjoyed the freedoms that allow us to make choices about our lives, including the choice to make the car our major means of transport and gasoline our top fuel. For nearly a century, these choices have helped create a standard of living that is the envy of the world. But now the whole world is paying the price.

The millions of passenger vehicles on our roads today are responsible for pollution, congestion, safety, and health problems. Exhaust emissions contribute heavily to global warming and acid rain, affecting the quality of life on Earth.

We must all act quickly to protect the Earth and the lives of all its inhabitants. Government and the automotive, oil, and recycling industries must cooperate, and each individual must respond so that we can develop a transportation system that will save our planet.

Chapter 8

Taking Action

EVEN IF YOU DON'T DRIVE, there are plenty of things you can do to help meet the environmental challenges presented by cars. Don't think that automobiles and their effects are not your problem—they are.

The pollution and congestion caused by cars affect us all, and we should be part of the solution. When we work together, we can make things change!

Perhaps the first step is, literally, a step! Actually, a whole lot of steps. Can you walk to places you want to go instead of driving or getting a ride? Maybe you could ride a bike or use public transportation.

Do you even need to make the trip at all? Could you accomplish your goal by using the telephone or a computer network? Maybe you can order things from a catalog, instead of driving around to shopping areas.

We can all begin by thinking about the role that cars play in our own lives and deciding to make that role smaller. Each time you get into a car, think about whether there might be a more environmentally friendly way to do what you need to do.

Driving Do's

If you decide that you must drive or get a ride in a car, there are lots of ways to make your trip better for the Earth.

If you don't drive, review the following tips and share them with drivers. And when you get your driver's license, be sure to practice what you preach!

If you do drive, remember that each time you drive, you are affecting the quality of life for everyone on the planet. Use your right to drive responsibly.

Buying Tips. The choice you make when you buy a car will affect the mileage you get and the damage you do to the environment for years. Here are some things to keep in mind.

• When buying a car, consider your needs and buy accordingly. Get the most fuel-efficient car possible, with only the options that you truly need. Think twice—and then twice more—about whether you actually need an air conditioner and power accessories in your car.

• Make high mileage a top priority. Consider a car that uses an alternative fuel.

• When buying a used car, check to see if the catalytic converter, which reduces pollution, has been disconnected or removed by the previous owner. It is expensive to install a new unit.

Driving Habits. The way you drive your car can have a great impact on your mileage and your pollution. Follow these tips regularly, and soon they will become habits that you don't even need to think about.

• Accelerate your vehicle slowly except when entering high-speed traffic lanes or when passing. Rapid acceleration can increase fuel consumption by 2 mpg (0.85 kpl) in city traffic.

• Don't rest your left foot on the brake pedal or clutch when it should be on the floor, and make sure your parking brake is released. The slightest pressure can cause drag, waste gasoline, and significantly increase pollution.

• Drive as steadily as possible. Every time you pump the accelerator you use extra fuel, and every time you hit the brakes you kill the momentum that it took fuel to build. Use cruise control, if you have it, to keep running smoothly.

- Pull away slowly from a stop and gradually gain speed. Racing the motor with quick starts uses more fuel and wears down the tires.
- Slow down for stop signs and stop-lights by letting up on the gas pedal. Don't race up to stops and then slam on the brakes.
- Warm the engine for only a minute, and then accelerate slowly. Driving in the highest gear is most efficient if highway conditions permit. Don't exceed the speed limit. Driving at 55 mph (88 kph) saves about 20 percent more gas than driving 65 mph (105 kph), even if that speed is allowed on some highways.
- Shut off the motor while waiting for someone or when waiting for a long, slow train to pass through a crossing. A minute or more of idling time wastes gasoline.
- Use your air conditioner as little as possible. Air conditioning reduces fuel economy by as much as 2.5 mpg (1 kpl) in slow-moving traffic. Open your windows instead. In fast traffic, open windows add to the air drag on the car, reducing mileage, so it's best to just use the vents.

Careful driving will help save gasoline, so trips to fill up the gas tank may be made less frequently.

Maintenance. There are many things you can do to care for your car that also help the environment. Here are some suggestions.

- Be aware of any unusual noises. A knock or a ping could mean your engine needs a tune-up. A thumping noise may be a sign that the rear differential or universal joint is defective. Drum brake linings that are worn emit a squeaking noise. Keep your ears alert to aches and pains in the car.

115

Cars that are kept properly tuned use less fuel and emit fewer pollutants into the atmosphere.

• Trust your nose to tell you if there is something wrong. A leaking fuel line lets the odor of gas into your car. If a rubber hose under the hood comes in contact with a hot engine, you smell burning rubber. The odor of burning oil could mean the transmission is overheating. A hole in the tailpipe lets exhaust fumes enter the car.

• Get your air-conditioning system checked every two years. A car air conditioner may be prone to leaks because of the regular vibrations of the auto, so keeping it in good repair will help keep CFCs out of the atmosphere. The CFCs lost from car air conditioners cause 16 percent of the ozone-layer destruction. Make sure that the garage where the work is done uses CFC recycling equipment. Don't do it yourself.

• Check tire pressure at least once a month. Under-inflated tires can decrease fuel economy by as much as 1 mpg (0.4 kpl) for every pound (0.45 kilogram) the tire is low. Visual checks cannot determine under-inflation until the tire is about 25 percent under-inflated. Tires use 2 percent more fuel for each pound they are under-inflated.

• Get regular tune-ups and maintenance checks for your car, approximately every 5,000 miles (8,000 kilometers) or less. Keeping your car engine tuned according to the specifications in your owner's manual will improve performance and gas mileage. Worn spark plugs should be replaced, otherwise they can cause poor starting and poor mileage. Mileage is also reduced when brakes drag or fluids are low. The average car could increase its gas mileage by 6 percent with a minor tune-up.

• Change your car's oil every 3,000 miles or so, to keep it in peak performance. When you change your car's oil, be sure to dispose of it properly at an oil-recycling collection point. Many full-service gas stations have such a program, or they can direct you to a local collection point. Don't just dump used oil into a drain or sewer, where it can poison millions of gallons of groundwater. Unfortunately, this is exactly what millions of lazy car owners do.

The amount of motor oil improperly discarded in the United States each year is 10 times greater than the amount of oil spilled off the coast of Alaska by the *Exxon Valdez* oil tanker in 1989. More than 1 million gallons (3.8 million liters) of waste oil are dumped like this each day!

FACT

• Take your old tires to be recycled. Larger vans and trucks can use retreaded tires. Retreaded tires are safe, long-lasting, and much less expensive than new tires—and they keep old tires from clogging landfills.

• Wash your own car. The automatic car wash uses too much water. At home, drive your car onto the lawn to hose it down. The water will then seep into the soil instead of running down to the street sewer.

• When adding gas to your car, do not "top off" the tank,

trying to get in a few extra drops. Most often, the excess just spills out of the tank anyway. This is an extra cost, as well as a pollutant in the environment.

• Get rid of excess weight in your car. Clean unnecessary clutter out of the trunk and interior. For every additional 100 pounds (45 kilograms) your car carries, gas consumption can increase as much as 0.2 mpg (0.085 kpl).

More Ideas. Changes in the ways and reasons you use your car can also have a positive impact. See if you can incorporate some of the following ideas into your life.

• Plan your travel to avoid congested roads and busy times. This will help eliminate stop-and-go driving, as well as idling time.

• Figure your mileage. Keep a record of the miles you drive and the gas you use for a few weeks to determine your average. Divide the total miles traveled by the total gallons used in order to learn your car's miles per gallon. Once you start using better driving habits, try this test again and see if your mileage has improved.

• When shopping, call ahead to make sure that the store has the items you want. Don't waste a trip. Combine several errands and plan the shortest route. Perhaps friends with errands to run can join you. It will save gas and make running errands more fun! Shop by phone when possible.

• If mass transportation isn't readily available, join or organize a car pool.

Express Your Opinion

Sometimes young people feel that their ideas and opinions are not respected by adults. But today's young people will have to live in the environment that adults are creating, so they should let their thoughts be known!

If road-building projects are going on in your town, look into them. How much land is being used? What will the roads do to communities they cross?

Consider the way traffic is handled in your community. Do cars often have to idle in traffic jams? What are the parking regulations? Are motorists paying full price for their parking privileges? Study issues like these, and consider their impact on the environment. Let your local officials know what you think should be done.

Make Your Voice Heard. National governments also play a key role in shaping the transportation systems of their countries. Learn what decisions your legislators are making and decide if you agree with them.

Keep up with news of changes and developments within the auto and fuel industries, too. Business leaders don't make money unless they give consumers what they want, so make sure your wishes are known. If a company is marketing a product or vehicle that isn't good for our Earth, let them know that you're against it. But also try to encourage companies with products friendly to our Earth, by buying their goods. Let them know why!

A good way to keep in touch with politicians and business leaders is by writing letters. Few people actually take the time to write, so every letter they receive carries a good deal of importance.

Following are tips that will help in writing to your government representatives, but most of the suggestions are useful in writing to business people as well.

Writing Letters. In writing a letter to express your opinion on controversial issues, follow these tips:

1. Make your letter one page or less. Cover only one subject in each letter.

2. Introduce yourself and tell why you, personally, are for or against the issue.

3. Be clear and to the point.

4. Be specific on whether you want your legislator to vote "yes" or "no" on a particular bill.

5. Write as an individual. The environmental group you belong to will have already let the legislator know its stand on the issue.

6. When you get a response, write a follow-up letter to re-emphasize your position and give your reaction to your legislator's comments.

State and Provincial Concerns. On issues concerning state or provincial legislation or to express your opinion about actions taken by a state or provincial environmental or natural resources agency, find an address at your library and write to:

Your local state or provincial legislator.

The governor of your state or premier of your province.

The director of your department of natural resources or similar environmental or energy agency.

Federal Concerns. On issues concerning federal legislation or to express your opinion about actions taken by the federal government, you can write to:

Your state's two U.S. senators. Check at your local library to discover their names. Write:

The Honorable _____
U.S. Senate
Washington, DC 20510

Your local congressman. Check at your local library to discover his or her name.

The Honorable _____
U.S. House of Representatives
Washington, DC 20515

Your local provincial or federal member of Parliament. Check at your local library to discover his or her name.

The Honorable _____
House of Commons
Ottawa, Ontario, Canada K1A 0A6

The President of the United States. He has the power to veto, or turn down, bills approved by the Senate and the House of Representatives as well as to introduce bills of his own. He also has final control over what the U.S. Environmental Protection Agency and other agencies do.

President _____
The White House
1600 Pennsylvania Avenue, NW
Washington, DC 20501

The Prime Minister of Canada.

The Honorable _____
House of Commons
Ottawa, Ontario, Canada K1A 0A6

Join Organizations

Many groups of people care about the environmental damage being done by cars. They are working to meet these challenges in many different ways. Some groups promote alternative fuels and means of transportation, while others try to improve our current methods. Many more check on environmental conditions around the world and inform the public of what they learn.

Association for Commuter Transportation, 808 17th St., NW, Suite 200, Washington, DC 20006

American Public Transit Association, 1201 New York Ave., NW, Washington, DC 20005

Center for Environmental Information, 99 Court St., Rochester, NY 14604

Citizens for a Better Environment, 111 King St., Madison, WI 53703

Environmental Action, 1525 New Hampshire Ave., NW, Washington, DC 20036

Environmental Defense Fund, 1616 P St., NW, Washington, DC 20036

Friends of the Earth, 218 D St., SE, Washington, DC 20003

Greenpeace USA, 1436 U St., NW, Washington, DC 20009

National Association of Railroad Passengers, 900 Second St., NE, Suite 308, Washington, DC 20002

Natural Resources Defense Council, 1350 New York Avenue, NW, #300, Washington, DC 20005

Rocky Mountain Institute, 1739 Snowmass Creek Road, Snowmass, CO 81654

Sierra Club, 730 Polk St., San Francisco, CA 94133

Transportation Alternatives, 494 Broadway, New York, NY 10012

Union of Concerned Scientists, 26 Church St., Cambridge, MA 02238

World Resources Institute, 1709 New York Ave., NW, Washington, DC 20006

Worldwatch Institute, 1776 Massachusetts Ave., NW, Washington, DC 20036

Everyone needs to be involved in solving the problems caused by gasoline-powered vehicles and by motor vehicles in general. There are many challenges, but if we work together, we can make the Earth a healthier place for generations to come.

GLOSSARY

acid rain – precipitation that contains a concentration of sulfuric acid, nitric acid, and other chemicals. It can cause great damage to the environment.

carbon dioxide (CO_2) – a chemical compound of carbon and oxygen. The main greenhouse gas, it is an exhaust emission.

carbon monoxide (CO) – a chemical compound of carbon and oxygen. It is an exhaust emission that causes human health problems and adds to the greenhouse effect.

catalytic converter – an insulated chamber containing various metal oxides, through which exhaust emissions must pass. It reduces the CO and HC pollutants.

chlorofluorocarbons (CFCs) – complex chemicals that contain carbon and chlorine. CFCs play a part in global warming by trapping heat in the lower atmosphere. But they also rise into the upper atmosphere where they damage the protective ozone layer.

crude oil – a fossil fuel from which petroleum products such as gasoline are formed.

emissions – particles or gases released into the air during the burning of fossil fuels.

ethanol – an alcohol compound that can be used as a fuel. It is most often mixed with other fuels to power cars, as it helps to cut greenhouse gas emissions.

exhaust – chemical by-products left over after the gas-air mixture is burned in a gasoline engine. It exits the auto as emissions.

fuel cell – An apparatus that releases energy when hydrogen and oxygen are combined within the cell. Electricity is released when water is formed during this reaction.

fossil fuels – crude oil, natural gas, and coal. These most-commonly used fuels formed over millions of years by compression and heating of partially decayed organic matter.

global warming – the gradual increase in the temperature of the Earth above the level it is normally kept at by the greenhouse effect. It is caused by the addition of carbon dioxide and other gases to the atmosphere, primarily from burning fossil fuels.

greenhouse effect – the trapping of the sun's heat within the atmosphere by certain naturally occurring gases such as water vapor and carbon dioxide, causing Earth's temperature to stay warmer than it would otherwise be.

hydrocarbons (HCs) – chemical compounds that contain hydrogen and carbon. They are a part of exhaust emissions.

hydrogen – an element that can be used as an alternative fuel. It causes very little pollution.

mass-transit – public transportation for large groups of people.

methanol – an alcohol made from fermented wood, coal, garbage, or gas that is used as a substitute for gasoline.

nitrogen oxides (NO$_x$) – any of several colorless gases composed of nitrogen and oxygen. They contribute to the greenhouse effect, and when combined with water, they form nitric acid, a component of acid rain. They are a part of exhaust emissions.

ozone (O$_3$) – a molecule made up of three atoms of oxygen. It is formed when sunlight acts on oxygen. In the lower atmosphere, it is a harmful part of smog. In the stratosphere, ozone helps prevent sunlight's damaging ultraviolet rays from reaching Earth.

particulates – tiny particles of ash, dust, and dirt that hang in the air, adding to pollution. Some particulates come from exhaust.

smog – urban air pollution made of exhaust emissions, smoke, and other gases.

sulfur dioxide (SO$_2$) – a pollutant caused by combustion of sulfur-containing fuels like gasoline. It contributes to acid rain.

INDEX

Bold number=illustration

carbon monoxide 34, 39, 40, 50, 51, 71, 72, 73, 89, 92, 96, 102, 123
carriages, horse-drawn 18, 25
catalytic converter 27, 38, 39, 77, 114, 123
cataracts 41
CFCs, see chlorofluorocarbons
China **85**
chlorofluorocarbons 40, 41, 116, 123
Chrysler Corporation 22, 68
cities **19**, 23, 25, **26**, 28, 47, 48, 58, 83, 86, 90, 94, 97, 98
Clean Air Act 53, 102, 109
climate change **40**
coal 34, 70, 72, 104
coke 107
Colorado 71, 72
commuter railways 94
commuters 47, 76, 83, 85, 89, 92, 94, 95, 96, 98
computer modeling **68**, 98
congestion, see traffic congestion
connecting rod 15, 17
consumers 101, 105
conveyor belt 21
corn 72, 73, 81
crankshaft 15, 17
crash tests 55
crops 40, 51
crude oil 34, 40, 42, 43, 74, 123
Cugnot, Nicolas-Joseph 13
cylinder 13, 15, 17, 33, 34, 35
Czechoslovakia 55

D
Daimler, Gottlieb 17
deaths, from accidents 53, 54
deaths, from auto emissions 50
dedicated use 70
Denmark 84
Denworth, Joanne R. 96
diesel engine 35
diesel fuel 33, 50, 73, 104
Doran **69**
Drake, E. L. **15**

driving habits 114
    Experience 30
drunk-driving laws 61
dual-fuel vehicles 70

E
East Indian Islands 15
Egypt 11
electric vehicles 14, 29, **66**, **69**, 74-77
electricity 17, 66, 69, 71, 75-78, 80, 81
electric-rail systems 91
electrolysis 79
electromagnets 95
elevated railways 90, **93**, 94
emissions 9, 27, 33-**35**, 40, 42, 43, 45, 50, 51, 53, 66, 70, 81, 86, 89, 96, 102, 105, 111, 123
    Experience 38
emissions reduction 71
emissions testing 35, **103**
energy 44, 108, 110
engine **16**
environmental cleanup costs 60
ethanol 72, **73**, 123
Europe 15, 52, 62, 84, **97**
exhaust 10, 33, 47, 109, 123; see also emissions
    Experience 38
Exxon Valdez **42**, 117

F
factories 8, 43
Federal Clean Air Act 27
federal funds 26, 97
federal government 110
fertilizers 72
flexible-fuel vehicles 70, 71
Flink, James 20
Florida **57**, 99
fluorine 41
flying 94
Ford, Henry 13, **14**, 20, 47
Ford Motor Company **12**, 22, 23
Ford Motor Company of Canada Ltd. 23

forests 52, **53**
fossil fuels 34, 42, 68, 69, 79, 92, 123
four-stroke cycle 15, **16**
France **62**, 94
freight train systems 94
Freon 41
fuel 34, 35, 66, 107; see also gasoline, hydrogen
fuel cell 80, 81, 123
fuel consumption 48, 49, 103, 110, 118
fuel efficiency 27, 28, 30, 68, 103, 114
future cars 68

G
garages 63
gas guzzlers 28, 30, **34**, 61, 105
gases 66
gasohol 72
gasoline 9, 14, 15, 27, **29**, 33-35, 38, 39, 42, 60, 65, 66, 68, 69, 71, 104, **115**
gasoline engine 15, 34, 77
gasoline pumps 29, 30
gasoline taxes 21, 61, 110
General Motors 11, 22, 75, 91
generator 78
Germany 22, 62, 95
global warming 39, 40, 41, **51**, 74, 111, 123
Gordon, Deborah 109
governments 26, 29, 60, 62, 68, 81, 91, 96, 109, 119
grain alcohol 72
grains 72
Greece 11, 51, 61
greenhouse effect 39, 123
greenhouse gases 39, 40, 72
groundwater 108
Guthrie, Woody 24

H
handicapped 59
hazardous wastes 38, 43, **45**, 109
haze 7

125

PHOTO SOURCES

AAA Wisconsin: 112, 116
American Academy of Science: 80 (top)
American Cancer Society: 41
Courtesy of the American Petroleum Institute: 14, 27, 29, 104, 115
Dr. Gary Benson: 11, 63, 97
Margie Benson: 50
Bike Centennial: 85 (bottom)
Bike Centennial/Gary MacFadden: 86
California Department of Water Resources: 40
Century Products Company: 55 (right)
Doran Motor Company: 69
Courtesy of the Drake Well Museum: 15
Ford Motor Company: 21, 45
From the collections of Henry Ford Museum & Greenfield Village: 12, 20
French Government Tourist Office: 62
General Motors: 55 (left), 64, 68, 71 (bottom), 75, 78, 103
Jeanine Hess: 6
Honda Motor Company: 71 (top)
Institute of Scrap Recycling Industries, Inc.: 32
Japan National Tourist Organization: 95
Jones & Thomas, Inc.: 73 (top)
Dr. William Lambert: 85 (top)
Los Angeles County Transportation Commission: 48
Mazda Motors of America: 80 (bottom)
Metro photo by Ned Ahrens: 2
Metropolitan Transportation Commission/Catalina Alvarado: 93 (top right)
Metropolitan Transportation Commission/Dennis Galloway: 90 (right)
Michigan Department of Natural Resources/David Kenyon: 100
Milwaukee Public Museum: 90 (left)
Photo courtesy of Ministry of Environment, Ontario, Canada: 108 (left)
National Propane Gas Association: 74
City of Orlando, Florida: 57
The Oxford Energy Company: 107, 108 (right)
Phillips Petroleum Company: 43
Alison Portello/The Davis Enterprise: 83
Regional Transportation Authority/Chicago: 93 (bottom right)
Photo courtesy of Ernie Rodriguez/Unocal: 105 (top)
Safety-Kleen Corporation: 105 (bottom)
Shell Canada Limited: 73 (bottom)
Greg Siple/Bike Centennial: 82
Solectria Corporation: 76 (left)
South Coast Air Quality Management District: 28 (both), 46, 66, 70, 89
State Historical Society of Wisconsin: 18
State of California/ Department of Transportation: 111
Dr. Donald H. Stedman: 35
Toronto Transit Commission: 24, 99
Dr. Louis Uehling: 9
United Nations-FAO 129070/G. Tortoli: 51
U.S. Coast Guard: 42
U.S. Department of Agriculture: 53
U.S. Department of Defense: 31
U.S. Department of Energy: 76 (right)
U.S. Department of Housing and Urban Development: 93 (top left)
U.S. Department of Labor: 26
U.S. Department of Transportation: 23
U.S. Department of Transportation/Federal Highway Administration: 19, 25
U.S. Department of Transportation/ National Highway Traffic Safety Administration: 56 (all)
Terri Willis: 34
World Bank: 10, 54

ABOUT THE AUTHORS

Terri Willis is an author and editor of several books and articles about the environment. Her work on the *SAVING PLANET EARTH* series includes *Land Use and Abuse*. A graduate of the University of Wisconsin—Madison, Terri lives in Lake Geneva, Wisconsin, with her husband, Harry, and daughter, Andrea.

Wallace B. Black, the co-author, is a dedicated environmentalist, writer and publisher. Along with Jean F. Blashfield, he is responsible for the entire *SAVING PLANET EARTH* series. He was also responsible for the creation of *THE YOUNG PEOPLE'S SCIENCE ENCYCLOPEDIA* and *ABOVE AND BEYOND, THE ENCYCLOPEDIA OF AVIATION AND SPACE SCIENCES*. He is a former pilot in the United States Air Force and is the author of a series of books on World War II.